D1525983

america's economy

1990 annual

David L. Bender, *Publisher*
Bruno Leone, *Executive Editor*
Bonnie Szumski, *Senior Editor*
Janelle Rohr, *Senior Editor*
William Dudley, *Editor*
Robert Anderson, *Editor*
Karin Swisher, *Editor*
Lisa Orr, *Editor*
Tara P. Deal, *Editor*
Carol Wekesser, *Assistant Editor*

greenhaven press, inc.

PO Box 289009
San Diego, CA 92128-9009

contents

Capital Gains Taxes Should Be Reduced

Ronald Utt

How to tax capital gains remains one of the most controversial issues confronting economic policy makers. Though a number of countries, like the Republic of Korea, do not tax capital gains at all, the United States approach has been a roller coaster. In the mid-1970s, for example, capital gains were taxed as high as 35 percent; this top rate was cut to 28 percent in 1978 and cut further to 20 percent by the 1981 Reagan tax reduction. Then the pendulum swung abruptly, and surprisingly, back in the comprehensive overhaul of the tax code in 1986. As a result, capital gains today are taxed at the same rate as ordinary income. This rightly alarms many economists because a high capital gains tax discourages investment, savings, and entrepreneurial risk-taking. Without these, the U.S. will become economically less competitive in the world.

Faulty Arguments

Opponents of capital gains rate reductions attempt to build their case on three arguments:

1) Equity and Fairness—Capital gains preferences, critics say, favor the wealthy by providing a disproportionate share of the benefits to upper income taxpayers.

2) Cost—A capital gains tax rate reduction is said to increase the federal deficit because it will reduce tax revenues.

3) Effectiveness—A lower capital gains rate, critics argue, will have little effect on the decisions of individuals to invest or engage in entrepreneurial activity.

Each of these criticisms is challenged by supporters of capital gains tax reductions. They marshal an extensive collection of facts and research to demonstrate that the opponents' positions either are exaggerated or simply untrue. In particular, the two capital gains tax rate increases and the two tax decreases since 1969 provide solid evidence how individuals, businesses, and markets respond to such changes. What the last two decades reveal is that investors, businesses and venture capital markets are sensitive to changes in the capital gains tax rate. The data show that when rates are raised, venture funding slows or declines; conversely, when rates are cut, the venture capital market spurts.

Many opponents of the tax cut will concede that the cut will create economically useful incentives, but they worry about the ostensible loss of tax revenues. Studies reveal, however, that these concerns are unwarranted. Detailed econometric studies of the record since World War II indicate that capital gains tax rate cuts actually generate tax revenues by encouraging individuals to invest in taxable assets, unlock realized and taxable gains and redeploy capital efficiently—generating taxable income.

Evenly Spread Gains

The evidence also indicates that the fairness concerns are misplaced. When income is properly measured, the data reveal that capital gains realizations are spread rather evenly throughout different income levels and do not accrue only to the rich. Indeed, households earning less than $20,000 accounted for more than a quarter of all capital gains reported by taxpayers in 1985.

Lawmakers considering legislation to reduce taxes on capital gains should examine this evidence carefully. Critics of tax cut proposals will level charges that a cut would be bad for the economy and the budget, and unfair to moderate and low-income taxpayers. Yet the data refute them, suggesting strongly that a cut would boost the economy while spreading tax benefits to all major income groups.

The debate over the wisdom of cutting taxes on capital gains begins with the very idea of whether the

Ronald Utt, "Capital Gains Taxation: The Evidence Calls for a Reduction in Rates," The Heritage Foundation *Backgrounder*, May 2, 1989. Reprinted with permission.

realized appreciation of any capital asset should be taxed. Many economists contend that such gains should not be taxed at all because they reflect either inflation or the market's assessment that a company's (or asset's) future earnings will be higher.

If the gain is in part due to inflation, then a capital gains tax serves to confiscate existing wealth accumulated from past income that already has been taxed at least once. Moreover, the tax, or penalty for inflation, is imposed only when the asset is converted from one form to another, thereby discouraging capital mobility and the efficient allocation of scarce resources.

Triple Taxation

When the gains reflect the market's reevaluation of the company's future profit potential, then the taxation of such gains, when realized, constitutes the triple taxation of income from capital: first when it is earned by the corporation and paid in corporate income tax; next when paid out as dividends and taxed at the shareholder's personal rate; and a third time when the gains are realized through the sale of the shares.

The tax code in the past has attempted to compensate for market reevaluation by providing special treatment for capital gains. For example: residential housing, which represents the single biggest investment for most households, is largely free of capital gains tax as long as the proceeds from the sale are reinvested in another residence, or if they represent a one-time cashing out of the investment close to retirement. Similarly, professional investors in income-producing real estate are able to avoid capital gains taxes through a technique known as a "tax free exchange of property." Investments in financial assets, however, have never been permitted this privilege, although the capital gains exclusion, which was an integral part of the tax code until 1987, reflected an inadequate attempt to do so.

"More new technology-based firms raise equity-type capital from private individuals than from any other outside source, including venture capital firms."

Absent appropriate tax exclusions, the gauntlet of taxation faced by investors discriminates against capital income, discourages savings and investment, and harms U.S. international competitiveness by raising the cost of capital for Americans relative to that of foreign competitors, many of whom fully exempt capital gains from income taxes. In fact, Belgium, Italy, Japan, The Netherlands, Hong Kong, Malaysia, Singapore, South Korea and Taiwan exempt all capital gains from income taxation, while long-

term (six months) capital gains in Germany are exempt. Meanwhile, effective capital tax rates in the U.S. have been increasing. The January 1989 *Economic Report of the President* calculates that the effective tax rates on investment in equipment due to the Tax Reform Act of 1986 quadrupled from 10 percent to 39.6 percent.

The Impact on Investment Decisions

Advocates of a reduced tax rate or an exclusion for capital gains contend that these changes would increase savings and investment by decreasing the cost of capital to a firm and increasing the return on investment to the investor. At present, the gauntlet of corporate income taxes, the taxation of capital gains, and personal income taxes creates a large gap between what business earns on an investment and what the individual shareholders ultimately receive. This gap often is referred to as the "tax wedge." Reduced tax rates would encourage individuals to acquire a financial asset by raising the after tax rate of return on the asset. Such rate reductions would make investments in new and growing firms relatively attractive because most benefits of such investments would be in the form of capital appreciation rather than income paid in taxable dividends.

For the firm, a lower capital gains rate would reduce the effective cost of capital and encourage the acquisition of productive assets. For the new and growing firm, with limited income but unlimited promise, a lower rate or capital gains exclusion would encourage investors to take risks by offering the opportunity for a potentially higher reward.

What the Data Reveal

Several studies and surveys on the effect of capital gains rates on the willingness of investors to acquire shares in new firms support the view that rate reductions have stimulated venture capital market growth. Although some analysts challenge this, arguing that a substantial portion of venture funding comes from non-taxed sources such as pension funds, the surveys and studies do not support this and instead indicate that the individual investor is an important participant in the venture capital market.

In a 1988 study by economists John Freear of the University of New Hampshire and William Wetzel of Babson College, questionnaires were sent to the chief executive officers of 1,073 technology-based ventures founded in New England between 1975 and 1986. The results from the 284 firms responding indicate:

1) More new technology-based firms raise equity-type capital from private individuals than from any other outside source, including venture capital firms.

2) Private individuals are the primary source of outside equity-type capital for new technology-based firms when total funds raised each time the firm goes to the financial market is under $1 million.

3) Private individuals tend to invest earlier in the

life of a new technology-based firm than do other outside sources of equity-type capital, including venture-type funds.

Significantly, an analysis of the ebb and flow of venture capital over time indicates that there is a close correlation between the availability of such funds and changes in the capital gains tax rate. . . .

Although the evidence strongly indicates that lower capital gains rates encourage individuals to fund risky ventures, many policy makers still question whether the benefits are worth the potential losses in tax revenues due to a lower tax rate on capital gains. Skeptics also believe that a lower rate of taxation bestows disproportionately greater benefits on higher income individuals than on moderate income Americans.

"Congress and the White House should work together to craft legislation to apply a lower tax rate to a broad definition of financial and tangible assets."

Proponents of a lower capital gains rate counter that, contrary to the intuitively plausible proposition that rate cuts reduce revenues, experience demonstrates just the opposite: every instance of a capital gains rate cut has been followed immediately by a significant increase in capital gains realizations (net capital gains proceeds received from the sale of assets and reported to the Internal Revenue Service) and by higher taxes paid on those gains. By lowering the tax cost of selling assets, and thereby increasing the after-tax yield on such assets relative to other sources, lower capital gains tax rates can lead to greater capital gains realizations and increased total tax payments by the owners of those assets.

Stimulating Investment

Lower capital gains rates, experience shows, also increase the attractiveness of such assets relative to other sources of income or consumption. This encourages more purchases of such assets, which bids up their prices, leading to higher realizations of capital gain when the assets are sold—both because there are more investors now holding such assets and because the increased demand raises their price and profits. Again, this rise in value and volume can mean higher tax payments even at a lower tax rate. And to the extent that such tax rate reductions stimulate more investment, business formations and entrepreneurial activity, then general income tax revenues also would rise.

The rate cuts of both 1979 and 1982 were followed by large increases in reported capital gains and by increases in capital gains tax payments. Conversely, the tax rate increase enacted in 1969 was followed by declining realizations and lower capital gains tax

revenues. Indeed, the $5.9 billion of capital gains revenues received in 1968 was not exceeded until 1976.

Some opponents of a cut in capital gains tax do admit that a rate reduction does boost immediate tax yields, but then they argue that the observed increase merely reflects a change in the timing of realizations that would ultimately occur at higher tax rates. Today's tax gains from a cut, they contend, simply would be at the expense of higher tax payments in the future under current rates.

Debate Heats Up

The primary focus of the debate over the capital gains tax is the predicted effect on tax revenues. As the debate has become more intense, the economic research on the subject has become more extensive and systematic, but unfortunately also more complex and arcane. Nonetheless, a review of the most recent studies suggests that the weight of evidence is shifting in favor of those analysts who argue that revenues will not decline if rates are cut. . . .

Closely related to the issue of revenues is that of fairness—who would receive the benefit of a rate reduction and how would this change their tax obligations. Few myths are as enduring as the belief that reductions in the capital gains tax rate shift the tax burden from the rich to the poor. Opponents of capital gains rate cuts assert that the rich would receive a disproportionate share of the capital gains realizations and most of the benefits. By their definitions, the critics note that the wealthiest two percent of the population receive more than a quarter of their annual income in the form of capital gains and that nearly 75 percent of all capital gains realizations are received by taxpayers with incomes over $100,000, while 45 percent of such gains go to those with incomes in excess of $500,000. . . .

Supporters of the rate cut respond that such tax rate reductions actually would increase tax payments from the wealthy because it would induce them to shift their wealth from tax shelters to taxable investments and to "unlock" gains that were not realized because of high taxes. The evidence supports this view. Past rate cuts have led to substantial increases in capital gains realizations and tax payments, and an increased share of these tax payments comes from upper-bracket taxpayers. Table 1 demonstrates this.

Table 1		
Adjusted Gross Income	Taxes Paid on Capital Gains ($ thousands)	Percentage Increase
	1980	1984	1980-1984
$0-20,000	422,097	574,917	36
20,000-75,000	1,847,440	2,543,912	37
75,000-200,000	1,915,221	3,478,397	82
200,000-500,000	1,443,513	3,405,787	136
500,000+	2,363,446	9,598,114	306

Source: Estimated by the Office of Tax Policy, U.S. Chamber of Commerce, using Statistics of Income, Internal Revenue Service.

As the table indicates, the tax payments by the richest segment increased more than eight times that of the lowest income group. Critics may contend that the rise in revenues merely reflects the improving stock market over the period, and that the largest single source of capital gains realizations are from the sales of common stock. But such a contention simply is not supported by the facts. Over the period covered in the table, the New York Stock Exchange Composite Index rose by just 36 percent compared with the 306 percent increase in tax payments by the richest income group. Revenue increases of this magnitude reflect increased unlocking of gains, proportionately more investment in taxable assets, and greater mobility of capital.

> "Tax payments by the richest segment increased more than eight times that of the lowest income group."

Table 1 also demonstrates that the cut in taxes actually shifted the tax burden toward the richest groups, in contrast to the popular wisdom. Between 1980 and 1984, the share of capital gains taxes paid by taxpayers earning $20,000 or less declined from 5.3 percent to 2.9 percent, while the share from taxpayers reporting incomes of $500,000 or more rose from 29.6 to 48.6 percent of all taxes paid on capital gains.

While Table 1 and analysis demonstrate the extent to which capital gains rate reductions lead to proportionately greater tax payments by the higher income households, such aggregate data as presented in Table 1 actually overstate the extent to which capital gains realizations are experienced by the wealthier households. In fact, capital gains realizations tend to be spread rather evenly throughout the income distribution when the income distribution is defined to include only "recurring" income—that is, reported income less capital gains realizations. . . .

Correcting High Tax Rates

The evidence accumulated since World War II makes a powerful case in favor of a substantial reduction in the capital gains tax rate. Whether the issue is encouraging savings and investment, fairness, or revenues, the data and the studies demonstrate that concerns expressed by critics of a cut are either unwarranted or exaggerated.

In response to this evidence, the White House and many members of Congress from both political parties have developed proposals and introduced legislation to rectify the mistakes made in the treatment of capital gains by the Tax Reform Act of 1986. While some of these proposals are better than others, collectively they represent a growing appreciation by public officials that low tax rates make important contributions to America's economic well-being. This trend should be encouraged and Congress and the White House should work together to craft legislation to apply a lower tax rate to a broad definition of financial and tangible assets.

Ronald Utt is a John M. Olin Fellow at the Thomas A. Roe Institute for Economic Policy Studies. As part of The Heritage Foundation in Washington, D.C., the Institute researches economic policy issues.

"While cutting capital-gains taxes is unlikely to increase government revenues or do much for investment, it will certainly succeed in redistributing income–to the rich."

viewpoint 2

Capital Gains Taxes Should Not Be Reduced

John Miller

Only in a supply-side world would a President propose a tax cut in order to increase government revenues. And only in trickle-down America would this President herald the cut as "tax reform" when 64% of the benefits are targeted to the richest 0.7% of taxpayers, while the bottom 60% of taxpayers would receive less than 3% of the largess. Yet this is precisely what George Bush is proposing with his capital-gains tax cut plan.

A capital gain is income from the sale of a personally owned asset—be it stocks, bonds, real estate, gold, or old paintings—that has gone up in value. With the Tax Reform Act of 1986, capital gains were taxed at the same rate as other income. But the Bush administration wants to exempt almost half of some categories of capital gains from taxation, claiming this will spur trading in financial assets, which in turn will lead to growth in tax revenues. Not only that, the Bush team argues that the tax break will trigger more long-term investment, helping to revitalize the economy.

There are a few things wrong here. Most evidence indicates that reducing taxes on capital gains will decrease tax receipts, not boost them. In addition, the tax cut is unlikely to have much effect on long-term investment—and particularly on the productive investments needed to rebuild the U.S. economy. That leaves one reason for the tax cut: to give the rich a bonus. A capital-gains tax break would so overwhelmingly benefit the wealthy that it would make the Reagan tax cuts of the early 1980s seem progressive by comparison.

The Bush administration is right that the capital-gains tax needs reform. But true reform would go in the opposite direction—closing old loopholes, not opening new ones.

John Miller, "Helping the Rich Help Themselves," *Dollars & Sense,* June 1989. Reprinted with permission.

Here's how the Bush proposal works. The proposal effectively cuts the capital-gains tax rate from 28% to 15%. Forty-five percent of profits from the sale of most assets held for three years or longer would be excluded from taxation. This means that a wealthy taxpayer with capital gains would pay a 28% tax on only the remaining 55% of the income from their long-term capital gains, or the equivalent of a 15.4% tax rate. Actually, the rate would be "capped" at 15%—the same rate currently charged on the taxable income of the poorest families. In a feeble gesture toward curbing speculation, the tax break would not exempt capital gains on real estate and art objects, nor gains on assets held for less than three years.

Significant Departure

Setting a lower effective tax rate for capital gains than for other income is not a new idea: capital gains were taxed at bargain rates continuously from 1921 to 1986. But the 1986 Tax Reform Act marked a significant departure. In return for dramatically lower personal income tax rates, the Reagan administration agreed to tax capital gains as ordinary income. As Vice President, Bush promised Congress that broadening the tax base to include all capital-gains income would provide the necessary revenues to offset the revenues lost from lowering tax rates on the wealthy.

Now, as President, Bush wants to keep the new lower personal income taxes for the rich and to reinstitute the preferential treatment of capital gains. The combination of the two would leave the tax on capital gains at its lowest level since 1942. At the same time, Bush asks us to believe that he can now increase revenues by reversing the very measures he argued earlier were necessary to maintain tax revenues.

The supply-side rationale behind Bush's revenue claim is simple, if fanciful. The supply-siders claim that if capital-gains taxes are cut, property owners will suddenly begin to sell previously hoarded assets. They point out that currently, there is only one way to beat the capital-gains tax: hold onto your assets until you die. When inheritors sell the property, they only pay taxes on capital gains that accrue after the date of inheritance. So, the argument goes, with gains taxes so high, substantial numbers of wealthy individuals have decided to hold onto their property for life—or at least until the tax rate drops. If the capital-gains tax was lowered, many of them would sell the property to realize the capital gains.

"In theory, property owners' increased willingness to cash in on capital gains could boost the total amount of taxable capital gains enough to offset the decreased tax rate."

In theory, property owners' increased willingness to cash in on capital gains could boost the total amount of taxable capital gains enough to offset the decreased tax rate. Bush administration projections hold that Treasury revenues would rise by nearly $5 billion in the next year (as capital gains increase 120%) and continue to grow for the following two fiscal years.

But in 1980, when presidential candidate Ronald Reagan made similar claims about the effects of cutting income taxes, George Bush denounced them as "voodoo economics." And today, almost no one outside the Oval Office agrees with the Bush administration's projections. If asset owners don't sell more, the annual loss to the Treasury from the tax cut would be $17 billion— increasing the projected deficit by almost one-fifth—and few tax experts believe that they'll sell enough to wipe out this loss.

For instance, two major non-partisan institutions of Congress examined the effects of the proposed changes in the capital-gains tax. The Congressional Budget Office estimated that the Bush scheme could lose from $4 billion to $8 billion a year. The Joint Congressional Committee on Taxation projected that while the proposal would raise revenues the first year, it would lose $13.3 billion over the next five years.

Nominal Increase

The history of capital-gains taxation offers confirmation that asset-owners' responsiveness to tax changes is not strong enough to justify Bush's optimistic revenue claims. After Jimmy Carter and a Democratic Congress lowered capital-gains taxes in 1978, stock sales rose in 1979, only to decline in 1980. And since 1986, when capital-gains taxes rose from 20% to 28%, capital gains have not decreased, but rather increased by more than 15% in nominal terms.

The Bush administration asserts that in addition to enhancing government revenues, a tax break on

capital gains would revive long-term investment in the 1990s—this time by affecting how the wealthy act as buyers. Lower taxes on capital gains would increase investors' rate of return, encouraging more investment and contributing to higher growth rates in the decade ahead. Because the tax cut applies only to gains on property held for three years or more, it allegedly would lengthen the planning horizon of investors. And with lower capital-gains taxes, owners of stocks supposedly would become more active traders, supplying capital to new, more productive uses.

But many in the business world find these arguments almost as far-fetched as the supply-side revenue claim—and progressives have even less reason to accept them. *Business Week* editorialized, "The issue is how to guide [the money of large institutional investors] into long-term investment. . . . It won't be easy, but tinkering with the capital-gains rate is like pouring buckets of water on a burning house." Other business interests have expressed alarm that cutting the capital-gains tax rate would lead to investment guided by tax avoidance, rather than by market conditions.

Instead of taxing capital gains at a lower rate than ordinary income, *Business Week,* the *Los Angeles Times,* and others have argued that investment can better be stimulated by adjusting capital gains for inflation before taxing them. They contend that inflation has discouraged long-term investment by forcing investors to pay taxes not only on profits but also on capital gains generated by inflation. With inflation indexing, investors would pay taxes only on their "real" capital gains, not on inflation.

Little Influence on New Investment

From a progressive viewpoint, both the Bush plan and the inflation-indexing alternative fall short as ways of encouraging productive investment. For one thing, both proposals overstate the influence of capital-gains taxation on new investment. These tax-cutting proposals seek to spark new investment by making new stock issues more attractive to investors. But the vast majority of stock sales affected by capital-gains taxes are not new issues but resales of existing stock, which generate no new investment. Furthermore, stock issues finance only a small fraction of new investment. In the 1970s and 1980s less than 10% of the money corporations raised from outside sources has come from selling stock. Even *Business Week* concludes that "the real problem in venture capital" is not that potential investors are deterred by the high tax rate on gains, but rather that there is "too much money chasing too few opportunities."

Since tax changes have limited effects on the volume of investment, the important question is whether they help to redirect the investment. Cutting capital-gains taxes across the board does nothing to direct capital to productive uses—such as plant, equipment, infrastructure, or education. But cutting capital-gains taxes selectively could affect the character of investment. By denying the capital-gains exemption to income from the sale of non-productive property, the capital-gains tax could discourage financial speculation and direct investment toward more productive uses.

Bonanza for the Wealthy

While cutting capital-gains taxes is unlikely to increase government revenues or do much for investment, it will certainly succeed in redistributing income—to the rich. Capital gains go almost entirely to the wealthy. The wealthiest 5% of all taxpayers receive 85% of capital gains; the richest 0.7% of taxpayers receive 70% of capital gains. Five of every six taxpayers with incomes of more than $1 million a year have capital-gains income, but fewer than one in every 20 taxpayers earning $10,000 or less have it.

Thus, cutting capital-gains taxes amounts to what Robert McIntyre, Director of Citizens for Tax Justice (CTJ), calls a "bonanza for the wealthy." CTJ estimates that about two-thirds of the benefits of the Bush cut would go to the richest 685,000 people in the nation, or less than 1% of taxpayers. These taxpayers, all with incomes over $200,000, would receive an average tax cut of about $25,000. For the 80% of families earning less than $60,000 a year the average tax savings from the Bush plan would be only $20.

The one-sided distributional effect of cutting capital-gains tax is reinforced in the Bush proposal by the fact it does not apply to the sale of homes, which qualified for the capital-gains exemption prior to 1986. As a sop for the less fortunate, the Bush proposal would allow families with taxable income of less than $20,000 to sell their homes tax free.

Fair Taxes Instead

A more progressive tax policy would stiffen taxes on capital gains, not cut them. On the national level, Jesse Jackson's "Budget Plan for Jobs, Peace, and Justice" included measures along these lines. Besides proposing to restore personal income taxes on the wealthy to their pre-1986 levels, the Jackson budget favored closing the loophole that allows the rich to avoid capital-gains taxation at death. This makes a lot more sense—and is far more likely to raise revenue—than countering the loophole by lowering gains taxes on the rich as Bush proposes. The Jackson plan also would have imposed a "securities-transfer excise tax" of 0.5% on the sale of certain kinds of financial assets, a tax that would reduce short-term speculative merger and acquisition activity.

Even some investors and economic theorists support such policies. Fifty years ago, John Maynard Keynes, the economist whose theories underpin much of modern economic policy, favored "a substantial securities transfer tax" to mitigate "the predominance of speculation over enterprise in the United States." On Wall Street today, Warren Buffet, the head of Berkshire Hathaway and arguably the most successful securities investor in America, favors "a confiscatory 100% tax on short-term capital gains"—taxing away all short-term gains to remove the incentive for speculation.

Increasing short-term capital-gains taxes has also found support in state and local governments. Since 1973, Vermont has imposed a short-term capital-gains tax on land sales in an attempt to slow the pace of development. Rhode Island also recently considered taxing short-term capital gains on real estate in order to curb housing speculation.

"A more progressive tax policy would stiffen taxes on capital gains, not cut them."

Both the Rhode Island bill, defeated by fierce opposition from the real-estate lobby, and the Vermont law contain several features that could be adopted in a progressive national capital-gains tax:

- To favor long-term investment, impose higher taxes on short-term capital gains, not lower taxes on long-term gains as Bush proposes.
- Define the short term in several different gradations subject to different tax rates, including near-confiscatory rates for the shortest term and most likely speculative investment. The Rhode Island tax proposal defined the short term to be 5 years and imposed tax rates ranging from 80% for six-month investments to 15% for investments held the full five years. The Vermont law has a similar feature and also mandates a tax rate that increases with the amount of profit, similar to the income tax.
- Specify the type of investment subject to the short-term capital-gains tax, directing the flow of investment away from speculative activity. The Rhode Island bill applied only to non-owner-occupied housing, exempting owner-occupied residences from the short-term gains tax.
- Use the revenues from the short-term capital-gains tax to fund domestic spending or non-speculative public investment. In the Rhode Island bill, tax revenues were to go to a neighborhood preservation fund.

Better than the Bush Proposal

Unlike the Bush proposal, these progressive alternatives would promote equality, raise revenues, and strengthen the economy. The burden of a beefed-up capital-gains tax would fall chiefly on those with incomes above $200,000, the same people who benefited most from the Reagan tax cuts. Furthermore, such a tax could be the first step toward a more explicit and progressive industrial policy, cooling speculation and directing investment into needed areas. Selective tax rates could guide resources into more socially worthwhile investments, such as education. Finally, the revenues raised from the capital-gains tax would provide funds to restore the cuts in domestic spending, or to reduce the budget deficit, or even to fund investment in publicly-owned industry. Instead of Bush's thinly disguised giveaway to the wealthy, we could have a capital-gains tax policy that would actually do us all some good.

John Miller is a member of the collective of journalists and economists that edits and produces the monthly Dollars & Sense *magazine, which offers commentary on current economic events from a socialist perspective.*

"A federal enterprise zone program, with its more powerful tax incentives, could have a decisive effect on the economy of America's inner cities."

Tax-Free Enterprise Zones Are Effective

Stuart M. Butler

It is heartening to see Congress apparently moving to take action to establish federal tax incentives envisioned in the enterprise zone idea, some ten years after the concept was introduced from Britain. While the early debate over enterprise zones did not lead to any federal legislation till 1987, when Congress enacted a very diluted form of the idea without the needed tax incentives, that debate did have two very important results that will help Congress now to craft effective legislation. First, it sparked an intense discussion over the nature of economic development in depressed neighborhoods. This discussion led to a much better understanding of the importance of small firms in job creation, and of the vital importance of community-based organizations in mobilizing local resources and talent. We now understand that if there is to be strong economic development in the inner cities, the core of business activity must come from small enterprises.

The second result of the debate in the early 1980s has been the passage in over 30 states of state-based enterprise zones. These state zones, beginning with Connecticut in 1982, have brought solid results despite the weak tax incentives usually available at the state level. The study of the New Jersey Enterprise Zone Program, the most recent analysis of a state, corroborates the general finding that well-designed state enterprise zones can have a significant impact on economic conditions in depressed areas. This body of experience at the state level bolsters the contention that a federal enterprise zone program, with its more powerful tax incentives, could have a decisive effect on the economy of America's inner cities.

With the bipartisan enterprise zone legislation introduced in the House in 1989 (H.R. 6) by New York Congressman Charles Rangel, and the similar

Stuart M. Butler, "How to Design Effective Enterprise Zone Legislation," testimony before the U.S. Senate Committee on Small Business, September 21, 1989. Published by The Heritage Foundation in its *Lecture Series,* © 1989. Reprinted with permission.

legislation introduced in the Senate by Minnesota Senator Rudy Boschwitz, we have at last an opportunity to enact strong and effective enterprise zone legislation to help revive the inner cities. But if the support for enterprise zones among congressional leaders and the Bush Administration is to lead to the best possible legislation, Congress must remember the debate of the 1980s and design a program founded on the fundamentals of urban development crystallized in that debate. This suggests that Congress should craft new legislation based upon four key principles.

1) Federal enterprise zones should spur local creativity, not attempt to micromanage local economic development.

The enterprise zone concept is based on the notion that even within very depressed areas there are resources—now often dormant or engaged in illegal activity—that can become the basis of legitimate new economic activity. Even in such blighted areas as the South Bronx there are underused or vacant buildings that could become the home of small firms. There are aggressive and creative community organizations that currently are able to mobilize the people to tackle the social problems that discourage enterprise. And there are in fact many small enterprises, either operating in the underground economy or engaged in illegal activity. By reducing the tax, regulatory, and other barriers to legitimate enterprise, these resources can be brought together in economic development for the benefit of the neighborhood.

Precondition, Not Panacea

In order to ignite economic activity, the enterprise zone programs should focus on establishing the best economic climate to foster entrepreneurship. This attractive climate, however, is a precondition for economic improvement and not the panacea. Other ingredients are required for economic development, many of them not strictly economic tools. Action needs to be taken, for instance, to tackle the staggering increase in drug use and crime within the inner cities: the National Drug Policy recently unveiled by the Bush Administration has a key role in tackling this deterrent to legitimate enterprise. Similarly the problems of the schools must be addressed, by introducing strong parental involvement through such devices as open enrollment and site-based management of schools. In addition, a policy for the inner cities must allow community-based organizations to take a leading role in providing services within the neighborhood, which in turn creates entrepreneurial opportunity and employment. That is one reason why HUD [Housing and Urban Development] Secretary Jack Kemp's strong support for resident management of public housing is so important. Similarly, heavy welfare dependence in the inner cities must be reduced through innovative welfare reform initiatives, such as those spearheaded in recent years by the states and made possible through waivers from federal regulations granted by the Reagan Administration.

Thus enterprise zones should be seen not in isolation, but rather as an economic dimension to a general strategy of stimulating creativity and empowerment in the inner cities. Enterprise zones are but one vital ingredient in what should be seen as a new war on poverty, where blighted urban neighborhoods are the first battlefield.

Urban Frontier

This emphasis on encouraging creativity by the "local troops" in the war suggests that federal policy in general, and a federal enterprise zone program in particular, should not try to micromanage initiatives in each neighborhood. Conditions are very different in different places. An approach that works well in one city may be ineffective in another. Thus we need to guarantee the highest degree of freedom for cities and their neighborhoods to experiment with new ideas to promote economic activity. Much like the frontier during the great movement west in America, where the remoteness of central government allowed creative local solutions to be applied to problems and opportunities faced by pioneers, the inner city should be seen as an "urban frontier."

This means an enterprise zone strategy should confine itself to establishing the best possible climate in incentives and barrier removal, and then allow those closest to the situation to design the details of the strategy. This means Congress should not load up an enterprise zone program with a wide range of well-meaning financial packages or finely-tuned incentives designed to promote particular kinds of ventures. Micromanaging the economy does not work in less developed countries; it does not work in America's inner cities. What government should do is establish broad, powerful stimulants to economic activity within a relatively simple framework, and allow a thousand flowers to bloom.

2) Congress should assure there is competition in the designation process.

There are some supporters of the enterprise zone idea who argue that federal enterprise zone incentives should be applied to any area that meets certain eligibility requirements. Such an "entitlement" approach would be a mistake. Enterprise zones should not be seen as federal manna from heaven, descending upon cities, but rather a federal dimension to complement a process of creative economic policy at the state and local levels. . . .

Thus I would urge Congress to stay with the principle that enterprise zone legislation should be seen as limited in its extent and in the number of designations, in order to encourage new approaches at the state and local level.

3) The zones must focus on small business.

Many state and local development officials continue to believe that the best way to assure economic growth in a poor neighborhood is to encourage large companies to locate there. They take it as self-evident that a firm employing 100 people must be better than one employing three. They also assume that progress is impossible unless a large firm is persuaded to become the nucleus or anchor for economic expansion.

In almost every instance this is an unwise strategy. The fact is that large firms are poor generators of new jobs. Research by David Birch at MIT [Massachusetts Institute of Technology] and others indicates strongly that it is small firms that are the primary generators of jobs in the U.S.—in fact the large firms in recent years have shown a loss of net new jobs. But large companies are not appropriate targets for another reason. Studies of location decisions of large firms indicate that chief among the factors influencing the decision are the availability of properly trained employees and an environment conducive to attracting and keeping skilled workers and managers. Tax incentives are well down the list of factors. . . .

"In order to ignite economic activity, the enterprise zone programs should focus on establishing the best economic climate to foster entrepreneurship."

Thus a federal enterprise zone program will be both expensive and largely ineffective if it seeks to recruit large companies to depressed urban neighborhoods. Instead the focus should be on creating the conditions necessary to generate new small enterprises, preferably drawn from the underused resources within the neighborhood itself. . . .

4) Tax incentives should stimulate small, start-up businesses.

This focus on new, small business creation as the foundation of an enterprise zone strategy suggests different tax incentives than we would use in a program aimed at larger firms. It also means that any enterprise zone program should reduce the costly burden associated with local regulation. If we are to foster the growth of small enterprises within large dilapidated resident neighborhoods, the program should encourage local authorities to streamline zoning, building codes, and other regulations and permits that can be an enormous obstacle to a small firm. Even simplifying the regulation process in the form of "one-stop shopping" procedures can be enormously beneficial by reducing the crippling cost of delays in obtaining appropriate permission.

In the case of tax incentives, the proprietors of small firms correctly point out that they lack the sophistication to use complex tax incentives. Thus, simple tax incentives are required. Owners also emphasize that their primary need is not reduction of taxes on profits—most make little or no profit in their early years on which to pay taxes. What they need are tax measures that will encourage investors and lenders to provide them with the long-term capital and working capital they need to start and develop their businesses. In addition, small firms, particularly those in high-risk depressed areas, tend to be chronically short of cash. Thus tax incentives to improve their cash flow, enabling them to take on labor and meet the other routine requirements of running a business, are crucial to success.

Two Forms of Incentive

This suggests that Congress should focus on two broad forms of tax incentive in a federal enterprise program:

A) Taxes on debt and equity capital. In order to provide an incentive for lenders and investors, Congress should consider the elimination of capital gains taxes for investments in enterprise zones. This would encourage investors to take the higher risk of putting their money in a depressed neighborhood, and it would encourage the proprietors of enterprise zone businesses to build them up over the long haul.

Such relief from capital gains taxes should not be restricted to certain types of investment. Restricting the relief, say, to investments in real estate development would shift economic activity away from less capital-intensive ventures that may in fact be more appropriate to the neighborhood. Trying to steer investment and loans to particular types of activity is just the kind of micromanagement that the enterprise zone program should avoid. . . .

B) Payroll taxes. Payroll costs are the other major obstacle for small firms in depressed neighborhoods. The Rangel-Boschwitz legislation addresses this by applying non-refundable income tax credits for certain types of employees. I suspect this may be the wrong mechanism. Making the employment credit non-

refundable certainly would reduce the immediate cost of the program and avoid breaching the principle of not providing cash subsidies to employers. But it would mean that small start-up businesses, which typically do not have profits on which to pay taxes, would have little benefit from the credit.

"The fact is that large firms are poor generators of new jobs."

Perhaps a better strategy would be to provide tax relief to the employee instead, by using enterprise zones as demonstration areas for an enhanced Earned Income Tax Credit (EITC).The current refundable credit would be both increased and linked to the size of the family, as many lawmakers and policy experts already have proposed in the context of welfare reform. This would mean more take-home pay for lower-paid workers, particularly for those leaving welfare or with large families. The employer would not need to be profitable for this non-refundable tax break to apply. Designing the employment tax relief in an enterprise zone, as a form of an expanded EITC, probably would be more effective than the current legislation's combination of non-refundable credits for both employer and employee.

This renewed interest in passing tax-based enterprise zone legislation is an important step forward in addressing the problems of depressed neighborhoods. The conditions in many areas may be far worse than when the concept was first proposed in the U.S., but there are also grounds to believe the concept might yield better results today. We have learned a great deal in the last ten years about the nature of the problem and the potential for various approaches. Pouring money into the inner cities has not succeeded in the past and there is little reason to believe it would do so in the future. Instead we should launch a strategy based on stimulating the dormant entrepreneurship within depressed areas themselves, combined with steps to empower residents to exercise greater control over their housing and education. Such an approach would be based on the knowledge we have acquired in recent years that improvement in a poor neighborhood can occur only if it is led from within.

Stuart M. Butler is director of Domestic Policy Studies at The Heritage Foundation, a public policy research institute in Washington, D.C., dedicated to the principles of free enterprise and limited government.

"This is the virtually unanimous conclusion of those who have studied state enterprise zones: tax incentives are relatively ineffective, and deregulation is a mirage."

viewpoint 4

Tax-Free Enterprise Zones Are Ineffective

David Osborne

In Jack Kemp's bosom beats the heart of an activist. Beneath his silvery perma-press coif lies the mind of a conservative. When the two get together—when the impulse to do something collides with the laissez-faire mindset—the result is inevitable: another tax cut. First came the supply-side cuts of 1981. Then the flat tax of 1986. And now come enterprise zones.

Kemp has argued that by virtually eliminating taxes and regulation in the inner city, we can spark a market-driven entrepreneurial renaissance. Now that he's Secretary of Housing and Urban Development [HUD], he may get to try it. The Bush budget includes $1.05 billion for enterprise zone tax breaks, spread over four years.

Unless Kemp radically revises his conception of enterprise zones, this will not be money well spent. I have argued elsewhere, in a book called *Laboratories of Democracy*, that we have a great deal to learn from the economic and social experimentation sweeping our states. In area after area, state governments have shown what works and what doesn't work. And in the case of enterprise zones, the verdict is in: Kemp's tax-driven version doesn't work.

This is not to say that enterprise zones can't work, or that Kemp is entirely misguided. He is right, for instance, to insist that poor areas will only improve when the market begins to work in their favor. But the conservative notion that we can create a healthy market simply by cutting taxes and regulations is simplistic. In areas that already have low rents and low wages, how much of a difference are low taxes going to make? Such communities also have sagging infrastructures, poor housing, and a shortage of educated, skilled workers—not to mention crime, drugs, illiteracy, and welfare dependency. To create a healthy market, this entire constellation of social pathologies, unskilled labor, and inadequate services

must be altered. And if that is to happen, government must play a central role.

This is the virtually unanimous conclusion of those who have studied state enterprise zones: tax incentives are relatively ineffective, and deregulation is a mirage. The keys to success are active development strategies, involving business, government, and the local community.

The Freeport Solution

The idea of enterprise zones is an import. Peter Hall, a socialist professor in Great Britain, proposed it after a look at the low-tax, low-wage vitality of Hong Kong. Hall suggested "freeports" in the worst areas of the inner city: small enclaves free of taxes, regulations, customs controls, duties, and a minimum wage. It was Hall's version of a "Hail Mary" pass: things looked bleak, nothing else had worked, so why not try something truly audacious—an attempt "to re-create the Hong Kong of the 1950s and 1960s inside inner Liverpool or inner Glasgow."

Margaret Thatcher pushed the idea through, in modified form. A British economist at The Heritage Foundation, Stuart Butler, sold it to Jack Kemp, who sold it to Ronald Reagan. In Washington the issue sank into ideological stalemate. But 30-odd states went off and tried it on their own. Today they boast between 500 and 700 zones, with at least as many designated but not yet operational.

Studies of these areas leave something to be desired; you never know exactly what would have happened had the zone not been created. Still, various studies have come to remarkably similar conclusions. Two studies each in Connecticut and Maryland found no impact. Studies in Illinois and Louisiana found little change. A study of Indiana's "most successful" zone found genuine progress, but its authors attributed the success not to tax and regulatory incentives but to the aggressive recruitment work, backed by hefty training and infrastructure grants, of

David Osborne, "The Kemp Cure-All," *The New Republic,* April 3, 1989. Reprinted by permission of THE NEW REPUBLIC, © 1989, The New Republic, Inc.

the publicly funded organization that manages the zone. This finding was reinforced by an in-depth analysis of 90 enterprise zones, conducted by Rodney Erickson of Penn State. He concluded: "One of the key factors that bridged across all of the high-performance zones was a strong, pro-active development policy."

The Failure of State Zones

The general failure of tax-driven zones hasn't kept state officials from lauding them. Connecticut offers a good example. Frequently cited as the best state program, it provides property tax abatements, a 50 percent corporate tax break for firms hiring disadvantaged workers to fill 30 percent of their new jobs, training funds, grants of up to $1,500 for new jobs created, small business loans at low interest rates, and miscellaneous other incentives. The state claims the program has created or saved 10,000 jobs.

A reality check is useful here. When *Business Facilities* magazine checked employment figures after four years of zone operation, it discovered that while the overall state economy had boomed, the zones had lost 250 jobs. When the Citizens' Research Education Network surveyed a third of all businesses in the Hartford zone, it found that only 12 percent were aware of all the incentives available and none had used any of them.

"When Business Facilities *magazine checked employment figures after four years of zone operation, it discovered that while the overall state economy had boomed, the zones had lost 250 jobs."*

Bridgeport has Connecticut's most active and most successful zone, according to HUD. By 1985 this program had a staff of three full-time professionals and an annual budget of more than $150,000. State officials boast that it attracted $33 million in new investments during its first five years. But when University of Illinois Professor Earl Jones compared zone investments and rehab activity during the first two years with those in a similar but unzoned area of Bridgeport, he found no difference. And a 1986 HUD case study found that not one businessperson who had received zone benefits said they were "the principal motivating factor in making a particular investment decision."

Massachusetts, just north of Connecticut, is one of the only industrial states without a zone program. Yet it is widely and rightly believed to have accomplished more in turning around its declining urban centers than any other state. Why? Because it has what business needs: capital, skilled labor, access to good markets, relatively low crime rates, and a state government that has been creative and aggressive in

its development strategies.

Pennsylvania offers another contrast. Richard Thornburgh, now Kemp's colleague in the Bush Cabinet, was the only governor in America who created enterprise zones but eschewed the Kemp tax-driven model. Thornburgh built a program that offers $250,000-a-year grants to communities that create comprehensive development strategies, then gives them priority in all other state grant and bond programs. Pennsylvania did add a few small tax incentives after several years, but they are hardly the heart of the program. Not surprisingly, Erickson's study rated Pennsylvania's program among the most effective in the nation.

Congress passed a bill in 1987 that would allow HUD to do much the same thing as the Pennsylvania government: designate 100 zones and target federal resources there. Kemp will decide whether to pursue it.

Why are state tax incentives so insignificant? For one thing, state business taxes rarely account for more than five percent of a business's expenses, so even deep cuts don't turn many heads. Advocates of federal enterprise zones argue that federal tax breaks, being larger, would do much more. But that's far from clear. An extensive literature demonstrates that taxes are quite low on the list of factors that influence business location decisions. (And a more recent literature indicates that regulatory environment is relatively insignificant.) A General Accounting Office study asked employers in two Maryland zones to rate the importance of various factors in their latest location decisions. "Financial inducements" came in 12th out of 13. The top four factors listed were "market access," "community characteristics," "site characteristics," and "government cooperation."

Even business leaders, though hardly averse to low taxes, admit that they're almost never decisive. John Sloan, president of the National Federation of Independent Businesses, which surveyed small businesses in 85 cities, said, "Far more important considerations, especially for the labor-intensive retail and service concerns that zones must attract if they are to cut unemployment significantly, include access to capital and a qualified labor pool, immediate market viability, adequate police protection, and affordable insurance. From these viewpoints, depressed areas offer companies nothing short of a hostile environment. No amount of 'less government' can create money, security, or a market where none exists."

The High Cost of Federal Plans

Neither surveys nor state-level experiments, of course, can tell us what deep federal tax cuts would do. But the British experience can give us a clue. There extremely steep cuts have succeeded in shifting some investment into enterprise zones, but the shift has come at great expense, and with very little payoff for the poor.

The British program virtually eliminated taxes on industrial, commercial, and retail buildings and drastically simplified zoning and permit processes for new buildings. It did bring significant investment into the zones, but 75 percent of that investment simply moved in from outside, thus further depressing surrounding areas. (And—as is always the case with such incentives—an unknown number of businesses got tax breaks for investments they would have made regardless.) The cost of creating those jobs that were genuinely new was, by one count, $67,000 per job.

The British example is a classic exercise in steering investment to a place, rather than to people. This is fine—though expensive—if the goal is to redevelop a place. A similar strategy has helped lure private investment back to Times Square in New York, for instance. It could also work to lure plants back to areas that have lost their manufacturing base but still have a skilled work force and an adequate infrastructure. In fact, the state zones that do work are in precisely these kinds of areas, according to Erickson.

This strategy may make sense if we decide it is better to subsidize firms to move into deindustrialized regions than to make the victims of industrial change pay the financial and emotional costs of moving elsewhere. But that is not Jack Kemp's purpose. He is talking about the inner city. And he is talking about stimulating homegrown entrepreneurship, not recruiting large firms. His target is the people in the zones. All our experience suggests, however, that by aiming at a place, he is likely to miss the people.

Focus on the Residents

The problem is simple. Deep tax incentives may shift investment geographically, but they cannot change the way the market works. In or out of zones, companies still need skilled, literate employees—and no amount of tax incentives can entice firms to hire people who can't reach the required levels of proficiency fairly quickly. (Purdue economist James Papke found that zone residents got only 6.3 percent of the manufacturing jobs created in Indiana's ten zones.) Meanwhile, the zone residents who don't get the new jobs nonetheless have to pay higher rents when real estate demand drives up rates. Poor residents—and sometimes struggling businesses—can even be forced out of the neighborhood when landlords begin rehabilitating properties, just as in any other gentrification process.

The distinction here is between economic growth and economic development. Growth is simply an increase in output. Development is a process through which people, communities, and firms increase their capacities to produce, creating an upward spiral that has its own momentum. Rural Southern states such as Arkansas and South Carolina experienced significant growth from 1950 through 1975 by recruiting branch plants from the North. But they did nothing to change the capacities of local people and communities, and when the plants moved overseas or closed in the late 1970s and '80s, they left behind devastated economies. To paraphrase Kemp adviser Paul Pryde, development is what happens in Japan; growth is what happens in Kuwait.

"Deep tax incentives may shift investment geographically, but they cannot change the way the market works."

Fortunately, we have a growing body of state and local experience—little of it connected to enterprise zones— to tell us what does work in the inner city. The necessary elements include investment capital; management assistance for local businesses; infrastructure investments; improved services, such as crime control, housing, and education; significant job training and adult education; and efforts to help people on welfare get training and jobs. And it is essential that community members benefit not just as employees but as owners—through tenant co-ops, community organizations, and old-fashioned home and business ownership. The most powerful weapon is a development institution that can bring private investment into the community, make loans, work with business owners, and guide the development process to make sure local residents get the benefits. A model for this already exists: the Shorebank Corporation—a private development bank, subsidized by philanthropists, that has turned around a poor black neighborhood on Chicago's South Side.

Even the father of American Enterprise Zones is now persuaded that tax cuts alone won't work. "One of the things we've learned is that you don't just declare a zone open and expect things to happen," says Stuart Butler. "You have to go in and use zone incentives as an advertising tool, and also as a good base on which to build other kinds of strategies. Working with community-based organizations to address a lot of social problems within the zone—crime and that kind of thing—seems to be very important." Paul Pryde agrees: "Federal tax breaks are necessary but in no fashion sufficient. A zone that has federal tax breaks but doesn't have a lot of state and local commitment, doesn't have the attention of the mayor and development officials, where the zone isn't marketed and managed creatively, isn't going to work."

Revised Ideas May Work

Could a Kemp bill embody a comprehensive proactive strategy? The fact that Butler and Pryde are among his advisers bodes well. All they have to do is convince him to modify his thinking on the subject. Under such a revised approach, federal tax breaks would be the bait used to convince state and local governments to pursue comprehensive strategies. The declaration of a federal enterprise zone would be recognition both that an area was impoverished and that state or local officials had fashioned a program capable of changing that.

Grants could serve the same purpose, of course, and waste far less money. It's true, as conservatives note, that grant programs can fall prey to pork-barrel politics, but exactly the same tendency afflicts selectively distributed tax incentives. This is a moot point, though: Kemp is not going to abandon supply-side economics anytime soon. Tax incentives it is.

"The last thing we want is venture capitalists and commodity traders moving their four-person offices into zones to take advantage of capital gains tax breaks."

If these incentives were crafted carefully—to help poor people rather than poor places, and to minimize the amount of money wasted on investments that would have been made otherwise—they could play a moderately constructive role in their own right, aside from their role in guiding state and local governments. For instance, tax breaks could be limited to companies that hired a significant percentage of poor zone residents. (The last thing we want is venture capitalists and commodity traders moving their four-person offices into zones to take advantage of capital gains tax breaks.) The breaks could also be denied to any firm moving from a distressed area outside a zone into a zone.

Kemp is getting advice from some of the right people, and the evidence they'll present to him is clear. The question is whether he will listen. Stay tuned. In an otherwise dull administration, the battle between Jack Kemp's heart and Jack Kemp's mind should be worth watching.

David Osborne writes about social and economic issues. He is the author of Laboratories of Democracy, *published in 1988.*

The Budget Deficit Is a Serious Problem

Charles L. Schultze

Since 1983, the nation has been unable to muster the political consensus needed to deal decisively with the immense federal budget deficit. One of the reasons is that the public and the Congress are faced with three quite different and conflicting views about the economic consequences of persistent large deficits.

One view often heard on Wall Street, in international financial circles, and among some economists is that continued failure to reduce the U.S. budget deficit threatens to cause an economic crisis, characterized by a plummeting overseas value of the dollar, soaring interest rates, and a severe recession exacerbated by financial disturbances.

In marked contrast, several prominent economists and public opinion makers have recently been arguing that the problem of the budget deficit has been vastly overstated and that excessive concern about it is getting in the way of addressing more serious economic and social problems. Here the left of center finds common ground with the supply-siders of the far right. Robert Eisner, Robert Heilbroner, and the left wing of the Democratic party join Jack Kemp, Arthur Laffer, and other supply-siders. Although they come from different analytic and ideologic backgrounds, they all arrive at a common set of conclusions deemphasizing the importance of the deficit.

Still a third viewpoint, shared by the majority of economists who have addressed the problem, and among whom I find myself, holds that the consequences of perpetuating large budget deficits will be neither explosive nor harmless. Rather, by reducing sharply the nation's already low rates of saving and investment, the deficits will slowly and almost imperceptibly but inexorably depress the potential growth of American living standards.

Charles L. Schultze, "Of Wolves, Termites, and Pussycats: Or, Why We Should Worry About the Budget Deficit," *The Brookings Review*, Summer 1989. Reprinted with permission.

In an economic bestiary, the conventional Wall Street view of the deficit might be characterized as the wolf at the door; the second view as the domesticated pussycat; and the third as the termites in the basement.

Is a Crisis Coming?

It is not at all inevitable that the maintenance of today's large budget deficits will bring on some kind of cyclical crisis. There *are* risks ahead that could be reduced if the deficits were smaller. Nevertheless, with competent management by the Federal Reserve, the United States can very probably continue to muddle through, maintaining economic stability despite high budget deficits, as it has done since 1983. Those who worry about a crisis, however, see one coming in the form of a "dollar strike." In this scenario, foreigners, observing that budget and current account deficits remain high, suddenly lose confidence in the U.S. economy and desert the dollar in droves. The dollar's exchange value plummets, import prices soar, and the U.S. price level rises sharply. To prevent this one-shot rise in the price level from pushing up wages and turning into a persistent and possibly accelerating wage-price spiral, the Fed has no option but to tighten monetary policy severely, raise interest rates sharply, and put the economy through the wringer of a recession.

This chain of events, while not impossible, is also not very likely. In the years ahead downward pressure on the dollar may well continue, but a precipitous dollar collapse is not at all probable. A failure by the United States to reduce its budget deficit would set off a dollar flight only if international investors began to think that the Federal Reserve might become unwilling to stomach the higher interest rates needed to neutralize any inflationary, excess demand effects of the budget deficit.

But since 1983 the Fed has had both the will and the political freedom to do the unpleasant things needed to deal with budget deficits much larger than those now in prospect. Moreover, at an unprecedentedly early stage of the recovery from the 1982 recession, it showed its willingness to push real interest rates far above their historical norms to keep the pace of expansion within bounds. And with U.S. interest rates already well above those in West Germany and Japan, a sudden plunge in the dollar would likely be self-limiting as dollar assets began to look more and more like a good buy.

All in all, the wolf-at-the-door thesis is not likely to prove out so long as the Fed continues to pursue a credible set of noninflationary policies—a quite reasonable assumption given recent history.

The Collapse of National Saving

That we may be able to muddle through, sustaining large budget deficits without a cyclical crisis, does not mean that the deficits do no harm and that we can ignore them. In addition to providing a stable prosperity today, a successful economy must also make provision for tomorrow. It ought to save a reasonable fraction of its income to invest in increasing the stock of productive capital in the hands of the nation's citizens. This accumulation of wealth will in turn contribute to the growth of national living standards.

Yet the national rate of saving and wealth has fallen substantially in recent years. And it is in this important aspect of economic performance that the high level of the federal budget deficit continues to damage the American economy.

"Had the United States been forced to rely only on its own saving, domestic investment would have fallen as sharply as saving did."

National saving consists of two major components—private saving and government saving. A government deficit represents *dis*saving, since an equivalent amount of private saving is absorbed in financing the deficit, leaving that much less available for national investment. The U.S. *net* national saving rate has fallen dramatically, from an average of 8 percent of national income during the first three decades of the postwar period to an average of 2.6 percent in 1987 and 1988. Both elements of saving declined. The private saving rate dropped by about three percentage points, to 6.4 percent in 1987-88. And dissaving from the government budget deficit rose to more than 5 percent in 1986 before falling back to just under 4 percent. That means that the United States has been on a spending spree throughout the 1980s, sharply raising the proportion of its income devoted to the combination of consumption and government

spending and correspondingly decreasing the fraction of income it saves for the future.

Had the United States been forced to rely only on its own saving, domestic investment would have fallen as sharply as saving did. But because the country was able to finance a major part of its spending spree by borrowing heavily from abroad, rather than by having to scale back investment here at home, net domestic investment in housing construction and business plant and equipment fell by less than two percentage points, compared with the 5 1/2 point drop in the national saving rate. As a result more than half of America's net domestic investment is now financed, directly and indirectly, from other countries.

Had the country adjusted to its lower private and public saving rates by radically cutting domestic investment in productive assets, the nation's productivity growth, which has already slowed, would have slowed even more, further depressing the growth of American living standards. But because we adjusted to the lower saving rate principally by borrowing from abroad, our living standards will suffer for a different reason—out of our future national income we will have to pay a continuing portion to foreign investors in the form of interest payments on the massive overseas debts we have been accumulating.

Two Scenarios

If we continue to consume this unprecedentedly large fraction of our national income—a fraction that is excessive in comparison either with our own history or with other industrial countries—the future can develop in two possible ways, neither of which is attractive. First, at today's high U.S. interest rates, foreigners might continue to find the United States an attractive place to invest some of their funds. The dollar would not fall, and the U.S. balance of payments deficit, after declining a bit more, would stabilize at a high level. The United States would continue indefinitely to borrow large sums from abroad, steadily increasing the future diversion of national income to overseas interest payments, and further depressing the future path of American living standards.

The second alternative is that foreign investors, despite high U.S. interest rates, might reduce their demand for dollar investments as they perceive a growing risk to the exchange value of their dollar holdings. In that case, the flow of foreign funds into the United States would decline. And then in corresponding amount, we would have to cut back domestic investment here at home to match our own shrunken national saving. The growth of U.S. living standards would suffer, not by further diversion of national income to overseas interest payments, but by a further slowing of the growth in national investment, productivity, and real wages. Either way, so long as the country overspends by running a large budget deficit in conjunction with low private saving, the future growth of the net incomes available to American citizens and their children will be gradually, but surely, eroded.

Making Molehills out of Mountains

Let me turn to the arguments which suggest that the federal budget deficit is not a serious national problem. To start with, a number of people quarrel with the way the budget deficit *or* private saving is defined. With a proper definition, so the argument goes, the national saving and budget deficit problems would be seen to be minimal.

One set of these views, generally associated with Robert Eisner of Northwestern University, comes from the left. There are four strings to Eisner's bow. First, he would adjust the budget deficit for the effect of inflation on the public debt. Because inflation reduces the real value of that debt, some part of the interest payments received by government bondholders—equal to the inflation rate times the public debt—has to be considered not as income to be consumed, but as an asset transfer needed to restore the real value of wealth and consequently to be saved. Under this view, the part of the deficit that is represented by the inflation adjustment is not income, does not increase demand for consumer goods, and does not lower the national saving rate. It should be subtracted from the deficit. If it were, the current deficit would equal 2½ percent of national income, not the 3½ percent commonly cited. By the mid-1990s the inflation-adjusted deficit would fall to about 1 percent of national income.

It may make sense to subtract the inflation adjustment when estimating the "true" size of the budget deficit, as Eisner suggests. But the whole question is irrelevant to the issue at hand. Making the inflation adjustment does not change the estimate of *national* saving one iota. If the inflation adjustment is subtracted from the deficit because it is not truly income to bondholders, than current statistics overstate not only the budget deficit but also the income and the saving of those same bondholders. The Eisner adjustment simply reallocates national saving among its components: less private saving, less government dissaving, with no net effect on national saving itself. Moreover, the inflation adjustment as a share of national income has recently been the same as it was on average between 1955 and 1980; the *increase* in the budget deficit since that base period, and its share of the responsibility for the decline in national saving, is just about the same whether the inflation adjustment is made or not.

Second, Eisner argues that some of the federal deficit finances the accumulation of public capital, which adds to the nation's productive wealth. On this account too the true deficit, excluding government capital formation, would be smaller than shown by the current unified budget deficit. To construct such a budget, one must not only subtract gross capital outlays from total government expenditures, but also add depreciation to other operating outlays. Excluding military weapons from the definition of productive capital, which I think is only reasonable, the federal government's net capital accumulation now runs at $7 billion a year—hardly enough to affect the measured size of the deficit. Net investment by state and local governments is larger—$22 billion in 1987. But that investment as a share of national income has fallen substantially since the pre-1980 period. Including such investment in the definition of national saving would magnify the size of the recent saving decline.

"There is indeed a practical limit to the speed at which monetary policy can effectively offset a shift in fiscal policy."

Third, Eisner and others say that because state and local governments are running a large surplus, the budget deficit for total government is much smaller than the deficit for the federal government alone. In fact, state and local governments are now running a small deficit in their operating budgets. As defined in the national income accounts, their budgets include the pension funds of state and local employees, which are large surpluses. Were these same employees in the private sector, however, those surpluses would be considered as part of personal saving; it is only a freak of the national income accounting system that treats them as part of the government budget. . . . In any event, no matter whether these pension fund accumulations are classified as private or as public saving, it does not change in one whit the measure of national saving and the fact of its collapse in recent years.

Fear of a Recession

A final point Eisner and others make is that a substantial reduction in the budget deficit would lead to recession, lower national income, and lower, not higher, saving. According to this view, it is unlikely that the policy mix could be shifted sufficiently toward monetary ease to offset the demand-depressing effect of fiscal restraint. That is reminiscent of Keynesian arguments from 30 to 40 years ago: "You can't push on a string with monetary policy." Whatever its validity in explaining events of the 1930s or the first postwar decade when the U.S. economy was flooded with cash, the argument is sheer nonsense in the current economic environment. *If* the economy were in a recession, *if* monetary policy were already quite relaxed, and *if* interest rates were at very low levels, then further monetary ease might be unable to offset the effect of a fiscal tightening. But the economy is at or close to full employment, and real interest rates are far above historical norms, conditions under which the old Keynesian fears of the inefficacy of monetary policy to stimulate demand are groundless.

There is indeed a practical limit to the speed at which monetary policy can effectively offset a shift in fiscal policy. The budget deficit ought to be eliminated not all at once but over a number of years. But I lose little sleep worrying that Congress and the president will suddenly agree on an excessively rapid reduction in the budget deficit—it is, to borrow a phrase from Senator Daniel Patrick Moynihan, forty-fifth on my list of fears, following right after my fear of being eaten alive by piranhas. . . .

Saving Targets

In the short run the saving rate fluctuates substantially, and that fact together with uncertainty about the causes of the 1975-85 downtrend make it difficult to predict the future course of private saving. Nevertheless, at a minimum, there is no warrant to believe either that favorable demographic trends will raise the saving rate or that a large part of today's low rate is a temporary aberration that will soon disappear. Until events demonstrate otherwise, the prudent course is to assume that the personal saving rate will continue somewhere near its present level.

If both the personal and business saving rates stay at roughly their recent level, total private saving will run at about 7 percent of national income, compared with a 9 1/4 percent average in the 30 years before 1980. What does this projection mean, then, for setting targets for the balance in the federal budget in the 1990s?

"We have no really powerful tools to raise the national saving rate to a reasonable level other than through eliminating the budget deficit and transforming it into a modest surplus."

Let me start by setting a very conservative, minimal target for national saving, namely, the rate of saving that—on its own without further reliance on overseas borrowing—would be needed to support enough investment to maintain the annual rate of productivity growth at its current level of 1 percent. The rate of growth in output per worker is determined by the pace of technological advance, the increase in workers' skills, and other similar factors, plus the amount of investment in capital goods. We have no evidence to believe that the pace of advance in technology, workers' skills, and other such factors will speed up. Given a continuation of the current rate of advance, we can calculate the specific amount of

investment, and therefore the specific amount of saving, that will be needed to maintain the current rate of productivity growth.

The saving rate required in the next decade or so to support the investment necessary to achieve this "business-as-usual" objective will not be as high as the saving rate for the decades before 1980. That is so for three reasons. First, the projected growth of the labor force is lower, so the increase in the capital stock necessary to equip the new workers is less.

Second, the pace of technological advance has apparently slowed since the earlier years, so the opportunities to invest profitably in additions to the stock of capital per worker are less. Third, according to the statisticians at the Department of Commerce, the quality-adjusted prices of computers and related equipment, which now constitute a large fraction of business investment, are falling rapidly, as the speed and capability of computers steadily increase. Each average dollar of saving now buys more capital equipment than it used to, producing more investment bang per saving buck.

Steady Productivity

To maintain the rate of productivity advance at its current pace, then, net investment needs to run somewhere between 5 and 5 1/2 percent of national income. And if the country is no longer going to rely on an inflow of foreign saving, it will have to save 5-5 1/2 percent of its national income to finance that investment. That investment rate is much lower than the 7.6 percent of national income devoted to domestic investment during the 1956-79 period. But it is much larger than the current national saving rate of 3 percent.

Even so, the business-as-usual saving objective is not ambitious enough by a long shot, because it does not take into account the demographic crunch that will come early in the next century when the baby boomers begin to retire and the ratio of retirees to active workers rises steeply. To avoid putting a major burden on the next generation of workers, the nation's saving, investment, and income growth should be increased over and above business as usual.

The magnitude of the additional saving needed is reasonably well represented by the growing annual surplus in the nation's Social Security and other retirement trust funds. The decision, taken in 1978 and 1983, to have this generation of workers pay for a larger portion of its own Social Security retirement benefits can be translated into economic reality only if the annual surpluses in the Social Security trust funds are used to increase national saving, the stock of national wealth, and the future level of national income above what would otherwise have occurred. In practical terms, that means national saving ought to be increased above the business-as-usual level by the amount of the annual surplus in the Social Security and federal retirement trust funds.

Allowing for some increase in payroll taxes to support hospital insurance under Medicare, which is not now fully funded, those surpluses should amount to about $2^1/_2$ percent of national income by the mid-1990s, which when added to the business-as-usual requirement of 5-$5^1/_2$ percent, gives a target national saving rate of about 8 percent. This more ambitious objective is approximately equal to the pre-1980 average.

Cut Spending, Raise Taxes

If the private saving rate is in the neighborhood of 7 percent, as I expect, then achieving an 8 percent national saving rate would require a government *surplus* of about 1 percent of national income, where the budget is defined to include Social Security. Without further action to raise taxes or cut government spending, however, a budget *deficit* of 2 percent of national income is likely out into the 1990s. Therefore, tax increases and government spending cuts amounting to some 3 percent of national income will be needed to achieve this conservatively defined set of national saving targets. And by the mid-1990s that will require almost $200 billion of budgetary actions.

You might ask why not try to encourage private saving with various tax concessions and incentives. But that is a loser's game. The payoff to such schemes is small, by the estimates of all but enthusiasts, and the revenue losses involved will end up raising the budget deficit by far more than they stimulate private saving, leaving behind a net decrease in national saving.

We have no really powerful tools to raise the national saving rate to a reasonable level other than through eliminating the budget deficit and transforming it into a modest surplus. In turn, I am absolutely certain that goal cannot be accomplished without a relatively substantial tax increase. Unfortunately, neither the American people nor their political leaders yet seem willing to accept one.

Charles L. Schultze is director of the Economic Studies Program at the Brookings Institution, which researches and publishes materials regarding current public policy issues. He is a former chairman of the Council of Economic Advisers.

"Something terrible may yet happen, but with each year in which it does not, the case for regarding the budget deficit as an economic crisis weakens."

viewpoint **6**

The Budget Deficit Is Not a Serious Problem

Jonathan Rauch

In 1985 the country's financial situation was a mess. The United States had embarked on an exercise in fiscal adventurism unlike any it had ever tried, outside wartime or depression, and the numbers looked shocking: from 1981 to 1984 the federal budget deficit had more than doubled, to a startling $185 billion, and the projections showed things getting worse fast. A new presidential term was just beginning; members of the policy-making establishment in Washington were resolved to put the budgetary fire out for good. (This should sound familiar right about now.) In the midst of this near panic over the deficit Charles L. Schultze, who had been the chairman of the Council of Economic Advisers under President Jimmy Carter, was telling anyone who would listen something that few people understood just then. "The tragedy," he said at the time, "is that there is no crisis." With any luck and some sensible management by the administration and the Federal Reserve Board, there would be no depression, no collapse, no caving in of the economic roof under the weight of the spectacular near-doubling of the national debt in only four years. The country could muddle through with these deficits for a long time, a possibility that Schultze, a fierce anti-deficit "hawk," acknowledged but fretted about.

Balanced budgets, it has been said, are the economic equivalent of chicken soup: whatever ails you, reduce the deficit. In the 1930s Herbert Hoover blamed the budget deficit for prolonging the Depression; in the 1970s people blamed it for inflation. Earlier in the 1980s people said that the budget deficit would drive up interest rates and abort the economic recovery, and that it would overstimulate the economy and re-ignite inflation; they have accused it of pushing up the dollar, and more recently of making the dollar weak. They have

said that it would certainly bring upon us a day of reckoning of one kind or another—a recession, a world financial crash, a big inflation, a crunching of the standard of living. Everybody waited. Nothing happened. The stock market crashed, but the economy glided on with eerie aplomb. The expansion, one of the longest of the postwar era, continued. Inflation stayed under control.

Gradually the wisdom of Schultze's words is coming home. Many professional economists have long agreed with Schultze about the deficit, albeit in a quiet, don't-mind-us-kind of way. The full import of what they were saying is at last seeping into the consciousness of the public and of the Washington political establishment. Something terrible may yet happen, but with each year in which it does not, the case for regarding the budget deficit as an economic crisis weakens.

A Weak Threat

Telling people that they had better balance the budget, or else, is fine—for a time. But it is like telling your son that he'd better stop smoking, or cigarettes will kill him: after a while, when "or else" hasn't happened, the deterrent effect of the warning wears off, and there is little to replace it. The credibility of the deficits-are-disastrous school is shot, which leaves everybody wondering what it is, after all, that we are so worked up about.

The President and Congress will soon be working on a package of deficit reductions, just as they have been doing since 1983—with some success: what were rapidly rising $200 billion deficits in 1985 are stable or slightly declining $150 billion deficits today. In Washington the anxiety level has decreased since 1987, partly because the worst deficits are behind us but also partly because, after several years in which the country broke every fiscal rule in the book and nothing terrible happened, it is harder to see why we had the rules in the first place. Conservatives and

Excerpted from "Is the Deficit Really So Bad?" by Jonathan Rauch, *The Atlantic Monthly*, February 1989. Reprinted with permission.

liberals have formed an unlikely alliance whose binding principle is that cutting the budget deficit is not, after all, the most important thing in life (they could, however, hardly be further apart on what *is* the most important thing in life). People in the middle, who have a gut feeling that what the country has been doing is wrong, are left to gnaw on a question: Is the deficit really so bad?

Maybe it is time to admit that running a big budget deficit is a survivable condition. Deficits do matter, a lot. But to see why they matter, one must use economics to look past economics, to the social compact. . . .

The Case for the Deficit

Hardly anybody actually likes deficit spending in prosperous times. But, as Herbert Stein, past chairman of the Council of Economic Advisers, has said, nobody likes open-heart surgery either. The question is, What's the alternative? On the Republican right many people have come to see deficits as less risky than any of the other available choices. On the Democratic left opinion has taken a similar drift in the past year or two. Conservatives would rather have deficits than bigger government; liberals would rather have deficits than smaller government. In the middle are those, like Schultze, who say that the first priority should be reducing the deficit and never mind about the size of government—but that middle has been shrinking as the deficits themselves have stabilized and set up regular housekeeping.

It used to be Republicans who shrieked about deficits and Democrats who said they were not such a big deal. Republicans have accused Democrats of turning around in their tracks on the issue and caring about budget deficits only after a Republican President started running them. There is something to that, although Reagan's deficits were unlike anything the country had ever seen before outside depression or war. If anything, the reversal of conservative Republicans was more striking. In 1981 Jack Kemp, who was then a congressman, announced, "The Republican Party no longer worships at the altar of a balanced budget." Conservatives were once people who instinctively felt that the budget should be balanced, even if that meant raising taxes. Now they are people who tend to believe that taxes should be held down, even if that means living with deficits.

They Don't Mind the Deficit

A good way to get inside their point of view is to visit Stuart M. Butler's office on Capitol Hill. Butler, a quick and forthright thinker, is in charge of domestic-policy studies at the conservative Heritage Foundation. Prominently displayed on his office wall is a framed picture of the economist Milton Friedman, beneath which is this quotation, from a talk Friedman gave in 1983: "You cannot reduce the deficit by raising taxes. Increasing taxes only results in more spending,

leaving the deficit at the highest level conceivably accepted by the public." Over the past decade or so that idea has become gospel to many conservatives, Butler among them.

"Like all public policy," Butler said in a recent interview, "it's a choice between alternatives. It's not that I love deficits. But I like to know what are the alternatives we're talking about. And the alternatives that have been proffered by Schultze and others I do not find attractive. I find them arguably leading to even less desirable economic consequences in the future. They open up, I feel, a political dynamic that might even be self-defeating"—that is, tax increases would be used to increase spending and not to reduce the budget deficit.

Butler and other conservatives argue that deficits are the symptom, not the disease. The disease is runaway federal spending. "There had been a rapid increase, prior to Reagan, of both spending and taxing. What Reagan has essentially done has been to top out or slow down the rising taxes. You had two runaway elements of public finance, spending and taxes. We've got control of one of them, taxes, and the deficit is the symptom of the fact that we haven't got control of the other. So the solution is to get rid of that other runaway item, which is the spending side. "

"On the Republican right many people have come to see deficits as less risky than any of the other available choices."

Suppose you offer Butler a deal: Reduce the budget deficit—say, by $100 billion—with a package that includes a substantial tax increase. He won't take it, even if you stipulate that all of the tax increase goes toward lowering the deficit and none goes toward increasing spending. "I think the negative impact on future generations of raising taxes would be higher than the impact of borrowing," he said. In other words, it may well be better for the economy, given the current burden of taxation, to continue borrowing than to raise taxes. The idea is that we are merely talking about subtle differences of economic effect when we choose between taxing and borrowing to finance the government, and it is not clear which is actually worse for the economy. Finally—and this is the argument that really infuriates liberals— conservatives believe they get something in return for the budget deficit: "I see the deficit as a wedge to put the pressure on public spending," Butler says. "If you're looking at the deficit and the size of the government sector, the second measure"—the size of government—"is far more important in its overall economic impact, and I think everyone who is in the conservative camp who is less bothered about deficits would pretty much agree with that line of argument."

So if in return for higher deficits we get a smaller government, it is a good trade.

Economics can't be used to prove Butler wrong, but there are certainly ample grounds for skepticism. Few economists would dispute that, everything else being equal, raising taxes is not generally good for the economy. The evidence is scant, however, for the proposition that raising taxes is worse than borrowing. We just don't know—and in such circumstances the usual presumption is that one ought to pay one's bills.

As for where a tax increase would go, some of it probably would be used to increase spending—but hardly all of it (the tax increases of 1982 and 1983, the latter a large one to keep the Social Security program solvent, played a major role in stabilizing the monster deficits of the early 1980s). Most people part ways with the conservatives in being willing to accept somewhat higher spending in exchange for lower deficits. Also, it is not at all clear that running deficits has held down government spending much. After all, the Reagan years set two postwar records simultaneously: for highest peacetime deficits (an average of 4.7 percent of GNP from 1982 through 1988, higher than in any preceding postwar year), and for highest spending (an average of 23.4 percent of GNP over the same period— again, higher than in any preceding postwar year). A lot of economists, many of them conservative, have long believed that *raising* taxes, not cutting them, is the best way to constrain spending in the long run, because it forces politicians to impose pain if they want to give out goodies.

Alas, the economic evidence is not strong enough to settle the argument. We do not know how big the government would have been without the large Reagan deficits, and we do not know how a tax increase or a like amount of borrowing would cascade through the economy to affect generations still unborn. And all of that is finally beside the point. If what you most want is smaller government or lower taxes, then budget deficits are a secondary concern. Something analogous may be said for the emerging thinking on the left, which turns the conservative argument on its head and says: A more aggressive government presence in the economy is vital to economic success, and if strengthening that presence means running a budget deficit, then so be it.

A Useful Deficit

Some economists on the left, including Robert L. Heilbroner, of the New School for Social Research, in New York, hold that large budget deficits are actually a good thing, as long as they stay under control. "When the economy needs stimulus, a deficit can be very useful," Heilbroner said. "Right now, I'm not terribly impressed by the overall rate of growth of the economy." These days, however, that position is rare. What is not so rare among liberals is the idea that there are three things we need to do for the national economy: avoid a recession; make additional investments in education, research, infrastructure (roads, bridges, and other public goods that have been allowed to deteriorate), and so on; and reduce the budget deficit. The budget deficit is third on their list.

"Liberals have traditionally worried more about unemployment than about inflation."

Jeff Faux, the president of the Economic Policy Institute, a new liberal Washington think tank, has become a leading proponent of this emerging liberal view. "I think deficits do matter," he said not long ago. "But I think that other things matter as well. The problem with the debate is that it has become dangerously oversimplified, as if all our problems could be resolved by simply erasing the fiscal deficit. I think that's wrong economically, and I think it risks what could be a very, very disastrous outcome—that is, a recession. It's not possible to have a recession next time. That is, if we have a downturn, it's going to turn into something worse"—because of the large amounts of debt hanging over the world financial system. "We're talking about a long economic bath for America, the likes of which we haven't seen since the 1930s."

Not everyone on the left goes along with Faux there, but liberals have traditionally worried more about unemployment than about inflation, and so they are generally averse to doing anything that they think might bring on a recession—which, as Faux points out, would just increase the deficit anyway, as tax receipts fell off and welfare spending rose. Faux and many liberals think that rapid deficit reductions could easily trigger a downturn. "Given the dangers of recession and what it can do," Faux said, "if you're going to take a risk, take it on the side of keeping the economy going."

Next on the priority list comes investment. Faux said, "We've got this sort of Catch-22. It's almost become a cliché that we've got to invest more, and we have to do that in order to make our economy competitive. But we can't do that because we've got this budget deficit, which in part is a result of our not being competitive. So we keep putting off what I think are these essential investments. At some point we have to realize that the neglect of certain public investments has gone on for so long that it's absolutely essential that we make those investments. When your tires run out, you need new tires." In effect, we can say that today's budget deficit makes our children worse off than they might have been—but how much worse for them still if we let the nation's stock of human and public physical capital fall into disrepair, or if the government fails to help us compete successfully with the Japanese. Suppose, then, that you offer Faux a deal: $100 billion, say, in new government spending on education, fighting poverty, building infrastructure, and the rest, all of which must be financed by borrowing and thus adding to the deficit. He would take it.

Recession and Inflation

Like the conservative argument, the liberal argument is credible but far from incontestable, and there are lots of grounds on which to question Faux's viewpoint. First, the big concern for most economists during 1989 has been not that a recession would start any minute but just the contrary—that inflation might be about to take off. If that is the case, then reducing the budget deficit would be just what the doctor ordered. Anyway, liberals, like conservatives, tend to overstate the government's effect on the economy: the deficit fell by $70 billion from 1986 to 1987, and nothing much happened at all. There is good reason to suppose that no deficit reduction that Congress might muster the will to pass would trigger a recession, especially since the Fed could offset some of the deficit reductions with lower interest rates.

> "The anti-deficit people who kept crying wolf, and who are still crying wolf, have done themselves and the polity no favor."

Second, and more fundamentally, the Achilles' heel of the liberal argument is inflation. In the past, efforts to keep the economy going at whatever cost have usually led to inflation, which then led to a recession when the Fed clamped down. To a large degree, that is what happened under Presidents Johnson, Nixon, and Carter. So, arguably, the liberals' plan does not prevent a recession, and might in fact bring one about. Liberals argue that a rapid inflation is now unlikely; many analysts on Wall Street say just the opposite; the truth is that nobody knows. Finally, practically no one disputes that borrowing is fine if it is used to make good investments. But the key word there is *good*. A lot of people—especially conservatives—look dubiously on the idea that the government will make good investments, given the pressures of politics, and they are very skeptical indeed that the government's investments will generally be better than the ones the private sector would have made had it held on to the money that the government, with its budget deficits, borrowed.

An Ideological Debate

Neither faction can prove its own economic assumptions or disprove those of the other side. Economics has produced no generally accepted answer to the question, What is the best mixture of taxation and borrowing by which to finance a given level of government spending? In the absence of an answer, people are using economic rhetoric to conduct a debate that economics cannot settle—a political and ideological debate over what it is that government should and should not be doing, and what risks are worth taking to achieve that goal. It was always so. The anti-deficit people who kept crying wolf, and who are still crying wolf, have done themselves and the polity no favor. They have tried to turn the fiscal-policy debate into a one-sided argument, to the effect that anybody who cared about the country's economic health had only one rational choice: cut the budget deficit. In the end they have undermined their own position by claiming too much, and have left the country confused and adrift on the question of why we make such a fuss about deficit spending.

Jonathan Rauch writes about economic and agricultural issues for the National Journal.

viewpoint 7

Increased Taxes Will Reduce the Budget Deficit

Herbert Stein

"Drug kingpin" is probably the worst label you can pin on anyone these days. But not far behind is "Tax Addict." The Republicans and Democrats are now locked in a struggle over how to raise $5.3 billion of revenue without earning that title. The Republican plan is to borrow the money from the future and call it revenue today. That is "Capital Gains Tax Reform." The Democratic plan is to confine the tax increase to a very few rich taxpayers and fudge it over with IRA [Individual Retirement Account] benefits for the more numerous middle-class.

It is all silly. We spent too much to buy these politicians to have them waste their time on $5.3 billion. That is about 3% of the federal deficit, one half of 1% of the federal revenues, one tenth of 1% of the GNP [Gross National Product].

Do We or Don't We?

If we don't need a tax increase we don't need any of that, and if we do need a tax increase we need a lot more than that. If deficits don't matter, we should give up struggling over $5.3 billion of revenue so that we would have more time to think about the Redskins. If deficits do matter they matter a lot more than $5.3 billion will fix.

In my opinion, we need $50 billion to $100 billion in annual new taxes. These will surely seem like outlandishly large numbers to most people. That is because the magnitudes with which we now live are not yet commonly appreciated.

I will give some examples of relevant magnitudes. The deficit-debt problem is large. In 1985 Congress and the president hailed the new Gramm-Rudman-Hollings Act as evidence of the nation's determination to reduce the deficit. The act laid out a target for reducing the deficit in steps to zero in fiscal 1991. These steps would have left a deficit of $532 billion

for the fiscal Years 1986 through 1990. Even on the administration's estimates for 1989 and 1990, the combined deficit for those years is going to be about $240 billion, or 45%, above the target. On a more realistic estimate the excess will be more than 50%. Moreover, the excess of the actual deficit over the original annual target is not diminishing. That excess was $47 billion in fiscal 1988. It will be around $90 billion in both fiscal 1989 and fiscal 1990.

The original Gramm-Rudman-Hollings targets were subsequently revised to postpone the achievement of the zero deficit until 1993. Hardly anyone thinks that with present policies that target will be reached. There is now talk of revising the act to postpone the date at which the balanced budget would be achieved until 1999, so that we can enter the next millennium with a clean slate.

There was some decline in the actual deficit after 1986. Much of that has been due to the decline of unemployment and the rise of the economy toward its potential level of output. The deficit has actually risen between 1987 and 1989, despite a rising economy. There is no sign that if the economy rises only along its potential path, the kind of policy we have been practicing will yield a decline in the deficit. And if there is a recession, as some day there will be, the deficit will rise.

In 1974 the federal debt held outside the Social Security trust accounts was 24% of GNP. Now it is about 42% of GNP. If the ratio of debt to GNP were now as low as it was in 1974 the debt would be about $900 billion less than it now is. If we were to balance the budget immediately, which no one expects, and nominal GNP rose by 6% a year, the present ratio of debt to GNP would gradually diminish. In about 10 years it would regain the ratio of 1974. Even if we continue to run deficits, but the deficits were of constant size, the growth of the economy would eventually reduce the ratio of debt to GNP. But if the deficit remains constant at the 1989 figure of $160 billion, and if nominal GNP grows by 6% a year, the ratio of debt to GNP will not regain the 1974 level until 2018. That is a long time off. And our children will be paying interest on the excess debt for all that time.

"Although $50 billion to $100 billion of additional annual revenue looks like an awfully large amount of money, in an economy with a GNP of more than $5 trillion it is not a daunting figure."

Although $50 billion to $100 billion of additional annual revenue looks like an awfully large amount of money, in an economy with a GNP of more than $5 trillion it is not a daunting figure. It can be raised without tax changes that are likely to have seriously adverse economic effects. For example, one might consider the following possible revenue sources, with their annual yields as estimated by the Congressional Budget Office:

• Eliminate deductibility of state and local taxes—$32.1 billion;
• Tax employer-paid health insurance as income—$25.1 billion;
• Raise premiums to cover 50% of the cost of Medicare Supplementary Medical Insurance—$18.6 billion;
• Limit the value of the mortgage interest deduction to 15% of the interest, the amount of the first-bracket tax rate—$14.5 billion;
• Increase the motor fuel tax by 12 cents a gallon—$11.7 billion;
• Tax 60% of Social Security benefits as income—$11.3 billion;
• Tax 30% of capital gains from home sales—$7.5 billion;
• Tax capital gains at death—$5.8 billion;
• Raise the tax on distilled spirits by 20% and raise beer and wine tax to the level of distilled spirits tax—$4.4 billion;
• Double the cigarette tax—$3 billion

That is $134 billion of revenue per year which leaves some room for making choices. On the whole, the incentive effects of these tax increases are more likely to be beneficial than harmful. And they do not involve raising income tax rates, which could probably also go up moderately without significant adverse effects on the supply of labor, capital or entrepreneurship.

Despite the economics of the case, the political argument against a large tax increase seems to be insurmountable. "The American people do not want a tax increase," we are told, and correctly. Neither do they want to go to the dentist, or cut down on smoking. But there is this peculiar and little noticed fact. In the last seven years of the Reagan administration, the government enacted, with Mr. Reagan's signature, tax legislation that raised the revenue in fiscal 1989 by almost $120 billion, according to estimates in the last Reagan budget. This consisted of the following legislation, with the amount of the resulting revenue increases:

• Tax Equity and Fiscal Responsibility Act, 1982—$55.7 billion;
• Social Security Amendments, 1983—$30.9 billion;
• Deficit Reduction Act, 1984—$27.7 billion;
• Budget Reconciliation Act, 1987— $13.9 billion;
• Miscellaneous other increases—$18.4 billion;
• Tax Reform Act of 1986—$24.4 billion;
• Miscellaneous other decreases—$2.6 billion.

These add up to a total of $119.6 billion.

Grand Total

Mr. Reagan retained his title as the world's champion enemy of taxes, despite all the tax increases enacted with his concurrence during his regime. He was able to pass this title on to his heir, George Bush. The lesson for politicians seems to be that you can get away with raising taxes if you talk as if you didn't do it.

In summary—a tax increase of $50 billion to $100 billion is not large relative to the size of our debt and deficit problem, relative to the amount that can easily be raised without adverse economic effects and relative to the amount that Mr. Reagan showed was politically acceptable.

Herbert Stein is a former chairman of the Council of Economic Advisers and a fellow at the American Enterprise Institute, an organization dedicated to researching and educating citizens about public policy issues.

"Raising taxes to balance the budget is rarely successful, and it undermines the economy."

viewpoint 8

Increased Taxes Will Not Reduce the Budget Deficit

Stephen Moore

For more than two decades, America's state governments regularly have been achieving the goal that continues to elude the federal government—balancing their budgets. In fact, while the federal government has run a budget deficit for each year since 1969, the states always have finished the fiscal year with a cumulative net surplus.

Despite this impressive record at the state level, federal policy makers continue to ignore the lessons to be drawn from state budgeting practices. For instance, most states have adopted powerful tools to check spending. These include balanced budget requirements (49 states), line-item veto power for the governor (43 states), and tax and expenditure limitations (26 states). Explains a study by the Advisory Commission on Intergovernmental Relations, "...the states have long had a good record of fiscal discipline, in large part because of [these] constitutionally and statutorily imposed limits on legislative and executive behavior." Yet Congress refuses to enact similar restraints, despite their proved effectiveness.

Powerful Arguments

Of all the lessons to be learned by looking beyond the Capital Beltway, perhaps the most important is that raising taxes to balance the budget is rarely successful, and it undermines the economy. In Washington, the chorus for higher federal taxes simply presumes that hiking taxes somehow will improve the economy by reducing the deficit, so lawmakers today are determined to force George Bush to abandon his "no new taxes" pledge. Yet the experience of the states argues powerfully against raising taxes. Those states that have kept taxes down have achieved more rapid rates of income growth, job creation, and business investment than their high-tax

Stephen Moore, "Taxes, Economic Growth, and Budget Deficits: What Washington Can Learn from the States," The Heritage Foundation *Backgrounder*, July 25, 1989. Reprinted with permission.

neighbors. The economies of Arizona, California, and until recently, Massachusetts surged during the 1980s; each cut taxes sharply in the late 1970s or early 1980s. Conversely, three of the slowest growing states—Iowa, West Virginia, and Wyoming—substantially raised the tax burden on residents during the same period.

This should be sobering economic news for the Washington pro-tax lobby. Just as high-tax states have lost jobs, businesses, and skilled labor to low-tax states, so the U.S. runs the risk of surrendering economic competitiveness to foreign rivals if Congress increases the tax burden. This danger is heightened by recent developments in Europe and the Pacific Rim, where many of America's competitors have cut tax rates to sharpen their competitive edge.

More Government Spending

Lawmakers have sought to defuse public criticism of tax increase proposals by pledging to use any new revenues to reduce the federal deficit. But once again, the track record of the states demonstrates that such pledges mean little. Over the past two decades, actions by states to raise taxes have resulted in higher spending, not lower levels of debt. States raising taxes have not improved their overall fiscal condition in the long run; rather, higher revenues simply have encouraged state legislators to vote for more government spending. The highly publicized fiscal crisis now confronting the Northeastern states is a dramatic case in point: Connecticut, Massachusetts, New Hampshire, New Jersey, and New York are struggling to avoid sinking deeper into debt. Yet the rise in tax collections in the region has outpaced the rest of the states by almost 25 percent since 1985.

Federal lawmakers thus should pay close attention to the experience of the states. If they do, they will learn two things. First, the federal budget deficit crisis is unlikely to be resolved by further increases in taxes. And second— even more important—they will

america's economy / 29

recognize that raising taxes could sound the death knell to America's seven-year economic expansion.

Ever since the early 1980s, when the nationwide tax revolt movement began to lose steam, federal legislators increasingly have argued that the U.S. is undertaxed. A common public perception encouraged by lawmakers in Washington is that Americans pay lower taxes today than they did in the 1970s and early 1980s, and that the federal deficit is rising because tax revenues have declined. The truth is that taxes have been edging upward at all levels of government, and by 1988, virtually all of the tax relief granted in the 1978-1982 period had been taken back by government.

"Ever since the early 1980s, when the nationwide tax revolt movement began to lose steam, federal legislators increasingly have argued that the U.S. is undertaxed."

The percentage of the American paycheck that is diverted to the coffers of government is back to the peak level of 1981. Thirteen separate federal tax hikes have been enacted since 1982, while tax revenues at the state level have been growing since 1986 at roughly twice the rate of inflation. As a result, tax receipts at all levels of government in 1989 will exceed $1.5 trillion—or about one-third of gross national product (GNP). According to the nonpartisan Tax Foundation, a moderate income ($45,000 a year) two-worker family will pay an estimated $14,000 in federal taxes in 1989. When state and local taxes are included, this family's total 1989 tax bill rises to about $20,000 a year.

Temporary Tax Cuts

As these data indicate, the tax revolt movement had only temporary success. The tax cuts of the late 1970s and early 1980s were only a brief interruption in the upward trend in taxation and the size of government.

Legislators in Washington and the states have built support for the recent wave of tax increases by insisting that the revenues would reduce government red ink. Several studies indicate, however, that a jump in federal revenues tends to be associated with higher, not lower, subsequent budget deficits. This is because Congress tends to regard higher revenues as an open invitation to spend more. A 1986 study in *Public Finance Quarterly* examined the relationship between taxes and deficits over more than a half century (1929-1982). Its chief finding: " . . . the causality tests leave no doubt that revenue increases lead to spending increases and not to smaller deficits.". . .

Many proponents of large tax increases to balance the budget also assume that such measures have little

adverse impact on the condition of the economy. Others, while acknowledging that progressive income taxes have negative economic effects, contend that taxes on consumption restrain consumer spending, promote national savings, and provide a convenient and relatively painless method by which the federal government can raise revenues. This reasoning has helped boost support for a wide range of consumption taxes, such as versions of a value-added tax, new gasoline taxes, and higher "sin" taxes on beer, liquor, and cigarettes.

Because of the diversity in their tax policies, the fifty states offer a fertile testing ground for examining the impact of taxes on economic growth. Much of the early research on state tax policy concluded that taxes were not a significant determinant of economic progress. Concluded one prominent study, for instance, " . . . empirical evidence that taxes affect interregional business location decisions is almost nonexistent.'' Yet more than a dozen studies conducted during the past ten years have produced very different results. The overwhelming consensus of these more recent studies is that the high-tax states have performed less well than low-tax states during the last three decades. This research has yielded a number of important conclusions. Among them:

1) *Incomes have grown fastest in low-tax states.*

In a 1982 study, economist Robert Genetski of the Harris Bank in Chicago compared taxes as a percentage of personal income in each state with income growth in the state. Genetski examined this relationship for the period 1963 to 1980. Although he did not find a systematic relationship between average tax burden and income growth, he did uncover "an inverse relationship between *changes* in state relative tax burdens and state relative economic growth." According to Genetski, "Those states with decreasing relative tax burdens tend to experience subsequent above average income growth. Those states with increasing relative tax burdens tend to experience subsequent below average growth.". . .

2) *Employment has grown fastest in low-tax states.*

States with low and declining tax burdens have created most jobs—particularly jobs in manufacturing and high technology industries. In a 1985 study, economists Michael Wasylenko of Pennsylvania State University and Therese McGuire of the State University of New York at Stony Brook concluded that between 1973 and 1980 the overall "tax effort" (taxes as a percentage of income) in a state had "a negative and statistically significant effect on overall employment growth and on employment growth in manufacturing, retail trade and services." In addition, the study found that sales taxes, which are widely assumed to have no effect on employment opportunities, in fact "had a negative and statistically significant effect on wholesale trade employment." The single exception to this general finding was where increased taxes were used to fund education; then the effect of taxes on economic growth was positive. . . .

3) *Rising state taxes deter business investment.*

Businesses tend to avoid states with relatively high tax burdens. In a 1985 study examining the period 1972-1978, Timothy Bartik of Vanderbilt University found that the plant location decisions of *Fortune 500* companies were significantly influenced by state tax policies. According to Bartik:

> A 10 percent increase in a state's corporate income tax rate (for example, from 4.0 percent to 4.4 percent) is estimated to cause a 2-3 percent decline in the number of new plants. A 10 percent increase in a state's average business property tax rate (for example, from 2.0 percent to 2.2 percent) is estimated to cause a 1-2 percent decline in the number of new plants. . . .These changes in business location patterns put some limitations on the ability of states to redistribute income away from corporate stockholders, both in state and out of state, and toward other state residents. . . .

The Example of the States

A 1985 report of the Advisory Commission on Intergovernmental Relations concludes that "similarities between the states and the national government argue for the general relevance of state experiences to the national deficit problem." Regrettably, Congress continues to bury its head in the sand by insisting that higher taxes are necessary to reduce the deficit and spur economic growth. Yet more than two decades of analysis of state fiscal policies shows that raising taxes slows long-term economic growth, encourages higher levels of government spending, and leaves the overall fiscal condition unchanged or worse.

It now appears that the availability of tax revenues is the only budget constraint limiting the size of government. With government now consuming more than one-third of gross national product, and taxes back up to their pre-tax revolt levels, the U.S. is at a critical point. The state experience shows not only that raising federal taxes further is likely to make the budget deficit picture worse, but also that it could derail nearly seven years of economic expansion.

Stephen Moore is a Grover M. Hermann Fellow at the Thomas A. Roe Institute for Economic Policy Studies. As part of The Heritage Foundation in Washington, D.C., the Institute researches economic policy issues.

"Before the balanced budget law, the budget deficit for fiscal year 1986 was projected to exceed $230 billion. . . . The law, however, immediately cut nearly $11.7 billion from the 1986 deficit."

The Gramm-Rudman-Hollings Law Is Effective

Phil Gramm, Warren B. Rudman, and Daniel J. Mitchell

Editor's note: The following viewpoint is in two parts. The first part was written by Phil Gramm and Warren B. Rudman. The second part was written by Daniel J. Mitchell.

I

Those who call the 1985 Gramm-Rudman-Hollings balanced budget law a bad law because deficit targets have been missed and accounting gimmicks have been used to avoid tough decisions would probably also suggest that religion is a failure because there are so few saints in the world.

Sure, the balanced budget law is not functioning perfectly from an accounting standpoint, but that misses the point. Critics fail to comprehend the purpose or effect of the law.

They focus on mechanism and minutiae when, in fact, the law represents a continuing commitment to deficit reduction. And the fact is that both the Federal budget deficit and Federal spending are lower than they would have been without Gramm-Rudman-Hollings.

Before the balanced budget law, the budget deficit for fiscal year 1986 was projected to exceed $230 billion and Federal spending policies had the country on the way to $300 billion deficits by the end of the decade. The law, however, immediately cut nearly $11.7 billion from the 1986 deficit.

Currently, the "great failure" of Gramm-Rudman-Hollings is to reduce the deficit below $117 billion—half of what the deficit was when we began. Moreover, the deficit, when measured against gross national product—which many economists consider to be more important than the actual dollar number—will be 60 percent lower in 1990 than it was in 1986.

Average annual real growth in Federal spending has dropped from 4 percent in the years preceding Gramm-Rudman-Hollings to 1.6 percent since.

In late 1985, most economists and many businessmen believed that a recession within the next four years was unavoidable. That recession has yet to materialize; the Gramm-Rudman-Hollings inspired change in Federal fiscal policy is at least partially responsible.

Affecting Specific Proposals

Too, the balanced budget law has dramatically affected specific legislative proposals which would have raised the deficit. In the fall of 1989 the Senate passed an amendment increasing anti-drug funding by $3.2 billion over the amounts previously agreed. That additional funding was fully offset with spending cuts in other areas. Can anyone imagine that happening before Gramm-Rudman-Hollings?

In 1986, during an election year, the Senate killed a $1 billion farm credit bill on a point of order created by Gramm-Rudman-Hollings. That same year, Congress enacted a revenue neutral tax reform law—something most Washington pundits had thought was impossible.

Finally, the defense budget, when measured in real terms, has declined in each of the last four fiscal years. Incidentally, both of us would have preferred somewhat higher spending on defense.

All of these actions are direct results of the Gramm-Rudman-Hollings law.

It is certainly true, albeit regrettable, that Congress and the Administration have resorted to budget trickery in order to avoid some hard decisions. And, while gimmicks to hide the true cost of Federal programs have existed for many years, we concede that the willingness of the two branches to resort to such tricks has increased somewhat in 1989.

Yet, even with the gimmicks, the deficit is projected to continue on its downward path in 1990.

Phil Gramm and Warren B. Rudman, "Deficit Reduction: A Love Story," *The New York Times,* October 25, 1989. Copyright © 1989 by The New York Times Company. Reprinted by permission. Daniel J. Mitchell, "Gramm-Rudman: A Potent Weapon for Spending Restraint." Reprinted from *USA TODAY MAGAZINE,* November 1989. Copyright © 1989 by the Society for the Advancement of Education.

If the across-the-board spending cuts that went into effect in October 1989 stick, Congress and the President will have failed in their work on the budget, but the deficit will go down.

If the necessary deficit reduction steps are taken to void the cuts, both the budget process and Gramm-Rudman-Hollings will be working. And it is noteworthy that, for all the concern expressed about the across-the-board cuts, nobody is talking about waiving them.

The Gramm-Rudman-Hollings law is a statement about our will and determination to confront the most serious economic problem facing our country — the Federal budget deficit.

Just as we don't judge the success of religion by the number of saints but by whether or not the world is better off, so should we judge Gramm-Rudman-Hollings.

II

As the battle over the budget drags on, many policymakers solemnly state that the deficit only can be reduced if taxes are increased. Democratic majorities in Congress and projections of slow economic growth supposedly add to the inevitability of higher taxes. It would appear that the White House is almost powerless to stop a tax increase.

Overlooked in this analysis, however, is the role of the Gramm-Rudman-Hollings Deficit Reduction Act. Most importantly, sequestration—the law's procedure for automatically restraining spending growth if the projected deficit exceeds the target by more than $10,000,000,000—is a powerful tool for the President. Unless Congress can muster a two-thirds vote to pass a tax increase over a presidential veto, George Bush can use a sequester to reduce the deficit without higher taxes. In effect, the President has the power to reduce the deficit without raising taxes, as he promised.

Few budget experts believe sequestration is the optimal outcome of the budget debate. However, as Federal Reserve Board chairman Alan Greenspan stated in testimony to the Senate Budget Committee in February, 1989, "it is certainly desirable, 1) to a tax increase, and 2) to especially doing nothing." The benefits of a sequester, especially when compared with the costs of higher taxes, far outweigh the imagined liabilities. . . .

Determining the Deficit Target

Gramm-Rudman already determines each year's deficit target. For 1990, it is $100,000,000,000 and will remain at that amount whether taxes are raised or not. Gramm-Rudman limits total spending in any one year to the sum of projected revenues plus the deficit target (plus a $10,000,000,000 "margin of error" for fiscal years 1990-92). More taxes simply allow Congress to meet the deficit target at a higher level of

spending. If it tried to enact a budget that spends more than Gramm-Rudman allows, sequestration would result, bringing spending back down to the sum of projected revenues plus the deficit target. (There is no $10,000,000,000 cushion with a sequester.)

The budget figures for 1990 demonstrate the taxes-spending relationship. The Administration estimates that tax revenues will total about $1,065 trillion if its budget is enacted. Since the deficit target is $100,000,000,000, this means total spending can not exceed $1,165 trillion ($1,175 trillion with the $10,000,000,000 cushion). What happens if Congress passes a $15,000,000,000 tax increase? Assuming, probably incorrectly, that the tax increase does not lower tax revenues by stunting economic growth, projected tax revenues would jump to $1,080 trillion. The Gramm-Rudman deficit target would not change, of course, so the limit on total spending would rise to $1,180 trillion ($1,190 trillion with the $10,000,000,000 cushion). A $15,000,000,000 increase in tax revenue would result in a corresponding increase in Federal spending.

The Administration has the power to fulfill the President's no-tax-increase promise. If the White House notifies Congress that failure to produce an acceptable budget will result in a sequester, lawmakers will have no choice but to comply or allow sequestration. Any effort to block a sequester, whether by repealing Gramm-Rudman or raising taxes, would require legislation, which the President could veto. So long as one-third of one house of Congress would be willing to sustain either veto, a very likely outcome, the President would win. This is one of the reasons why Congress has been willing to work with the Administration to produce a budget that reduces the deficit without taxes.

"Unless Congress can muster a two-thirds vote to pass a tax increase over a presidential veto, George Bush can use a sequester to reduce the deficit."

However, if it became apparent that the Administration was using the no-lose sequester strategy, opponents quickly would focus their attacks on sequestration itself. According to the critics, a sequester would mean deep and arbitrary cuts, threatening vital services and government programs, and would signal a breakdown of the political process, risking a panic in financial markets. Finally, a sequester would determine the defense budget, risking our survival as a nation.

Notwithstanding these strident accusations, a sequester is a reasonable way to reduce the deficit. A sequester does *not* mean deep and arbitrary cuts. A sequester lowers spending only in comparison to the Gramm-Rudman baseline, which is a projection of what 1990's spending would be if the budget were allowed to increase automatically. Federal spending actually would increase under a sequester by $14-20,000,000,000. Many of the so-called safety net programs, which are exempt from the sequester, would grow very rapidly. Defense spending, the area of the budget most affected, would fall by $10,400,000,000. Other budget categories would escape relatively unscathed.

"Should Congress refuse to enact a budget which meets the Gramm-Rudman deficit target with a more desirable mix of spending restraint, a sequester could be the best alternative."

Just as the sequester's cuts are not deep, neither are they arbitrary. Lawmakers deliberately chose what programs would be exempt from a sequester and which ones would not. At any time, legislators have the option of altering the formula that guides the sequester. Furthermore, Gramm-Rudman provides Congress an opportunity to modify a sequester. If some element of it were a serious threat to public health or safety, policymakers would be able to alter the package. . . .

Meeting the Target

Few people would list a sequester as their ideal budget. In the world of politics, however, decisions often must be made between two or more imperfect choices. Should Congress refuse to enact a budget which meets the Gramm-Rudman deficit target with a more desirable mix of spending restraint, a sequester could be the best alternative. It certainly would be better than a tax increase.

Phil Gramm is a Republican senator from Texas, and Warren B. Rudman is a Republican senator from New Hampshire; both are members of the Senate Budget Committee. Daniel J. Mitchell is a former director of tax and budget policy for Citizens for a Sound Economy, which seeks to maintain a sound economy by promoting free enterprise.

"The only success G-R-H [Gramm-Rudman-Hollings] has achieved is in perpetrating the hoax on the American people that the president and Congress are dealing with our budget problem."

The Gramm-Rudman-Hollings Law Is Ineffective

Anthony C. Beilenson

The budget agreement between President Bush and congressional leaders is supposed to produce a federal deficit of $99 billion in 1990. Don't believe it. The actual deficit will be at least $30 billion to $60 billion higher than that, even if all the spending cuts and revenue increases called for by the agreement are enacted.

The pretense about 1990's deficit isn't the fault of the budget negotiators; they did what the Gramm-Rudman-Hollings Act required them to do—or, more to the point, what it let them get away with doing. The problem is that we are operating under a law that encourages dishonest, irrational and irresponsible action on our budget problem.

Gramm-Rudman-Hollings, the highly touted scheme that Congress concocted in 1985, was going to solve our nation's deficit problem once and for all by balancing the budget in five years through strictly enforced deficit-reduction targets. If Congress didn't cut each year's deficit to the specified level, then "automatic" spending cuts would do the job for us.

The result? The deficits have gone up, not down, in 1987 and 1988. And the 1989 deficit, which was supposed to be cut to $72 billion by G-R-H, is instead going to be about $163 billion.

The huge gulf between G-R-H's promise and the actual results is usually attributed to the political gridlock that has stymied deficit-reduction efforts in recent years. But G-R-H itself has played a major role in our failure to do a better job of reducing the deficits. Had we not passed that law, we would be much closer to balancing the budget than we are today.

G-R-H has perverted the way the president and Congress approach the budget problem. Our objective is no longer to reduce the deficit; it is to avoid automatic spending cuts. Our energies are directed not toward cutting spending and raising taxes, as they should be, but rather toward doing whatever it takes to meet the coming year's deficit requirement. That encourages us to focus on short-term budget changes, rather than on sustained, long-term reductions in annual deficits. It also gives us an incentive to use all the gimmicks we can think of to show higher revenues and lower spending in the coming year's budget than our policies will actually produce.

One result has been our inability to enact sensible reforms that cost money in the short run but save much more money in the long run. And still another has been our incentive to hide spending at any cost—a perfect example of which is President Bush's $50 billion "off-budget" bond proposal to solve the savings and loan crisis. Financing the bonds off-budget will make it easier to comply with the G-R-H requirements, but it will add about $4.5 billion to the interest costs that taxpayers will incur over the next 30 years.

G-R-H also invites the use of optimistic assumptions about interest rates, inflation, and growth that allow the president and Congress to project a smaller gap between spending and revenues than will actually occur. The use of such assumptions is the main reason that the Office of Management and Budget was able to project a $145 billion deficit for 1989, when the actual deficit is likely to be $18 billion higher than that. This sort of phony budgeting existed before G-R-H but, because achieving the wrong deficit number now triggers automatic spending cuts, we now have a much greater incentive to use unrealistic economic assumptions.

Finally, G-R-H aims at a balanced budget, which seemed to be the right goal in 1985, but is increasingly viewed as the wrong goal in 1989. Most economists are now recommending that the government work toward a budget surplus, because $56 billion of this year's revenues, and much larger amounts in future years, consist of surplus Social

Security funds. These funds mask the true size of each year's deficit. They are, after all, intended to be saved to help pay benefits when the baby boom generation retires; instead, they are being used to pay for current expenses of other government programs.

G-R-H condones the use of surplus Social Security revenues for other purposes by counting these funds as regular federal revenues. Although nearly everyone in Congress agrees that it would be prudent to set aside and save these surplus revenues, G-R-H makes it impossible to do so, because we couldn't come close to reaching even our phony deficit-reduction targets without them: If we didn't count them, this year's deficit would be $219 billion, rather than $163 billion.

Still, G-R-H defenders say, this law has brought discipline to our budget process and put pressure on the president and Congress to reduce the deficit.

Has it?

When Congress can't meet the law's deficit requirements, we change them. That's what we did in 1987, stretching out the timetable for balancing the budget by two years to make it easier to meet the annual deficit requirements. This year's target, for instance, was eased by a whopping $64 billion-to $136 billion. And since we allow ourselves a $10 billion margin of error and use phony economic assumptions, we don't even meet the more relaxed requirements. So much for discipline.

As for pressure, the last time we approved new spending cuts and tax increases was after the stock market collapsed in October 1987. It was the howls from Wall Street—not the threat of automatic spending cuts—that got the president and Congress to act.

"G-R-H aims at a balanced budget, which seemed to be the right goal in 1985, but is increasingly viewed as the wrong goal in 1989."

What's worse, in that instance G-R-H was responsible for our failure to take advantage of a rare opportunity to make real headway on the deficit. Even though the crisis atmosphere had produced the right political climate for enacting larger reductions, we simply confined our efforts to meeting the law's arbitrary (and recently relaxed) deficit requirements.

When Congress created G-R-H, many members believed that it would succeed because it would provide both the president and Congress with justification, or cover, for enacting the unpopular spending cuts and tax increases needed to reduce the deficit. But just the opposite has happened: It has provided justification for not enacting those measures. In truth, the only success G-R-H has achieved is in perpetrating the hoax on the American people that the president and Congress are dealing with our budget problem. Before long, it won't even succeed at that.

Congress could do something really useful by repealing Gramm-Rudman-Hollings. Then the next time congressional and administration negotiators meet to forge a deficit-reduction agreement, they won't be able to hide behind phony, meaningless deficit targets again. Instead, they'll actually have to reduce the deficit.

Anthony C. Beilenson is a Democrat from West Los Angeles. He is a member of the House of Representatives and serves on the Budget Committee.

The Trade Deficit Is Serious

William R. Hawkins

Then the Gods of the Market tumbled, and their smooth-tongued wizards withdrew, And the hearts of the meanest were humbled and began to believe it was true That All is not Gold that Glitters, and Two and Two make Four—And the Gods of the Copybook Headings limped up to explain it once more.

Rudyard Kipling wrote the above lines in 1919, the year after World War I ended. The war had delivered a fatal blow to international laissez-faire. It had shattered the dream of classical liberals that interdependence would put an end to national conflict. The claim of J.B. Say, that as a consequence of his celebrated Law of Markets "[a]ll nations are friends in the nature of things," sounded rather empty to the veterans of the trenches. It well deserved a place in Kipling's critique of utopian liberalism.

England and the United States

The war had revealed England's weakened economy. The U-boats had nearly starved the interdependent island, while England's industrial capacity and financial reserves proved inadequate to sustain its position as a dominant power. Both Germany and the US had surpassed "free trade" England in industry at the turn of the century by creating large internal or otherwise politically protected markets. In the years before the war England had found itself in somewhat the same situation as the US today. British industries were blocked from exporting to most of the world by foreign mercantilist policies, yet its own empire was open to rivals. The US exported more steel to the overseas British Empire than did British firms, while British exports to the vast US market were restricted by tariffs.

World War I also made the US the world's largest creditor nation, a status it held until 1983. The center

William R. Hawkins, "Whose Wealth of Whose Nation?" *Chronicles,* January 1990. Reprinted with permission.

of world finance shifted to New York from London and the dollar replaced the pound as the world's key currency. The dollar still holds a central position, but the long-term prospect is not good. Continued large trade deficits will put downward pressure on the dollar, as will the shift in the net American flow of overseas investment income from positive to negative. A currency that is likely to drop in value makes a poor basis for a world economy. If policies do not change, the strong Japanese yen will replace the dollar by the end of the century. Already as a result of Japan's economic prowess, eight of the world's ten largest banks are Japanese. As of 1986, Japanese banks held 31.6 percent of all bank assets worldwide (the US held 18.6 percent). And every year that the trade imbalance continues, the financial situation worsens.

Free traders have dismissed the merchandise trade deficit by claiming that there can be no overall imbalance because dollars paid out for imports are recycled to the American economy as capital investment. This is true in a narrow accounting sense, but those who cannot look beyond their simple ledger sheets miss the bigger picture of the international realignment of wealth and productive capacity. Americans are consuming goods on credit, then selling off their assets to pay the bills. Such profligate behavior leads to a relative decline in favor of the creditors.

Foreign Investment

There are two basic categories of foreign investment: direct investment in the ownership of enterprises (FDI), and portfolio investment (FPI) in long-term financial instruments. Direct investment accounts for about one out of every six dollars of foreign investment in the US. The Commerce Department has estimated that at the end of 1988, 15 percent of American manufacturing was controlled by foreign-owned firms. There was a record inflow of $58 billion in FDI in 1988, compared to only $17 billion in US direct investment placed overseas. The main factor cited by Commerce in their 1988 report on international direct investment was the basic profitability and stability of the American economy. Yet the US has always been attractive on these grounds. What is different in the 1980's is that foreigners have lots of dollars to invest, thanks to the trade deficit and dollar devaluation. Another worrisome factor, this one cited by Commerce, is that foreigners "are becoming increasingly confident in their ability to compete with US firms in the United States."

"American society is far more interested in present consumption than future growth."

At the moment, the US economy (due to its vast size) is less influenced by FDI than are many other host countries. However, the effects will accumulate like those of a slow leak. It took the *Titanic* two and a half hours to sink after hitting the iceberg. Pointing only to current figures while ignoring the trend, which is what many free traders do in regard to investment flows, is like reporting after the first half hour that since the ship is still afloat there is nothing to worry about.

Some foreign investors are very ambitious. Masaaki Kurokawa, head of Nomura Securities, has predicted that California will become a joint US-Japan community based on Japanese money and managers and American land and labor. So enthusiastic is Kurokawa that he has even claimed that California will cease to be considered part of America. This is farfetched, perhaps, but economic imperialism has a long history. The United States has used it to influence events in foreign lands, so why do American leaders believe others will not?

The shift in investment flows marks a waning of American wealth and power. During the 1975-80 period, the US was the source of 44.2 percent of the world's international direct investment funds. In the 1980-85 period this dropped to 19.3 percent. During the 1982-87 period, US firms acquired $23.4 billion worth of foreign companies, but foreign firms bought up $101.9 billion worth of American companies. State governments in the US know where the money is today. More states have offices in Tokyo than in Washington. Several states have been very aggressive in courting FDI, hoping for local gains even at the cost of undermining the national economy.

Market Extensions

Often it is said that it is better for foreign firms to produce in the US than simply to export goods produced overseas to the American market—that at least the factories, jobs, and tax base are in the US. There is some truth to this—at least the argument recognizes the damage done by imports—but it is not the whole story. It overlooks the role of FDI as a market extension strategy, as a way to penetrate overseas areas. About one-third of exports to the US go to foreign affiliates in the US; components to be assembled in production, capital equipment and supplies, even the materials and personnel to build the facilities themselves originate abroad. These American affiliates are "hollow" or "beachhead" corporations. As they expand, so does the trade deficit. American-owned affiliates overseas play the same role in boosting US exports. This is why a shift in the balance between American and foreign multinational firms affects the domestic economy so strongly. As the market share of foreign business empires expands, the market share remaining for American firms shrinks. And since foreign firms have access to low-cost capital (the cost of capital in Japan is half that of the US), they can at present expand when American firms are unable to.

Victory in these commercial struggles cannot be a matter of indifference to governments. As Princeton's Robert Gilpin reminds us in his *Political Economy of International Relations*, the corporations that operate in the world arena

> are not truly multinational; they are not divorced from a particular nationality. Home governments not only have the incentive but also may have the power to fashion commercial and other policies designed to benefit their own multinationals at the expense of competing firms and other economies.

The money involved in foreign portfolio investment is even greater than in direct investment. Private FPI accounts for 60 percent of America's $1.5 trillion (and growing) foreign debt. It grew at an annual rate of 50 percent between 1980 and 1987. Over this period, foreign activity shifted from Treasury securities to corporate bonds to the stock market and back. In 1985, bonds of American corporations sold overseas equaled one-third of the bonds issued publicly in the US. In 1986, foreigners bought 25 percent of all the newly issued US corporate equities, as well as 15 percent of all newly issued corporate bonds. In 1987, the inflow of private FPI roughly equaled all individual savings generated by Americans.

Narrow Focus

Free traders argue that the influx of capital boosts domestic economic growth, and this is true. But again their focus is too narrow. The dollars start and end in the US, recycled through foreign hands. Would it not be better if this capital stayed in the US to begin with, earned by American firms selling in the domestic market and reinvested by and for Americans? The problem is as much cultural as economic. American society is far more interested in present consumption than future growth. Both private and public spending levels rest on debt, with a growing dependence on foreigners for financing.

This is economically unsustainable and politically unwise. A saturation point will be reached. A slowdown in the US economy, a political crisis, the onset of inflation or a further slide in the dollar will increase the risk to foreign holders of dollar-denominated assets. If the country is still dependent on foreign borrowings when that happens, the result will be higher interest rates and a dramatic slowdown in the domestic economy.

To pay off debt and interest charges, the US will have to return to a trade surplus or suffer the downward spiral of accelerating asset sales. The market solution is massive dollar devaluation to cut imports and boost exports. However, this also reduces the terms of trade, so that an even larger transfer of real goods and assets is required. Debts are claims against future income, and current policy is making these claims larger.

Curtailing Imports

The proper solution is to end both the trade and budget deficits. Either a tax increase or a budget reduction would accomplish this, though the second is preferable. The private sector cannot stand a further shift of resources to government if it is to recover the ground lost to foreign competitors. Indeed, tax cuts to encourage savings and investment are vital elements of any industrial policy. The reduction in aggregate demand necessary to solve the debt problem should be managed at the expense of imports. It would be self-defeating to slow the domestic economy by taking the hit at home. That means intervention to curtail imports so that 1) domestic demand can be maintained even as its aggregate drops, and 2) the country can move to a trade surplus without gutting the dollar.

"The proper solution is to end both the trade and budget deficits."

The US also needs to escape its dependence on foreign capital for political reasons. A "globalized" capital market is likely to become more sensitive to international tensions and crises. And from this will come greater pressure on the US to avoid conflict through appeasement. In the past, the nervousness of allies and neutrals over confrontations or military operations has been expressed in diplomatic terms that a determined administration could politely ignore. But if that nervousness can now be expressed by a drop in the stock market, a jump in interest rates or factory lay-offs, with the distress this will cause among the business community and domestic electorate, any administration will become even more

wary of taking strong action. Foreign firms have already organized their American employees to campaign for policies that favor their interests, while millions of dollars are funneled to candidates, former officials, and think tanks to influence decisions. Given the pacifism of our allies and trading partners in Europe and Japan, the danger is not just that America's enemies will control its economy, but that its friends will. Indeed, the "peace in our time" rhetoric from the Reagan-Bush White House over the last five years may already be a sign of this.

A Great Power

Such an inhibition would be the negation of Great Power status. A Great Power by definition is one that has the freedom to act unilaterally, to take as little or as much of the outside world as its interests dictate. The kind of economic interdependence now being promoted would have the same effect on the United States that being tied down by the Lilliputians had on Gulliver.

The relative decline of the United States and the diffusion of power across a multipolar globe bodes ill both for Americans and the world at large. It must be remembered that what stability there has been during the last half of this century has been due to the preeminence enjoyed by the US since its triumph in World War II. As William R. Thompson noted in his study *On Global War*,

> The more pronounced and unambiguous the postwar hierarchy of prestige, as reflected in the dominance of the leading power, the more likely the system to enjoy a period of peace and stability. . . . Their decline, however, creates situations of conflict and instability.

There has been a world economy for five hundred years, but it has not depended on anything as dubious as an "invisible hand." The stakes are too high. It is national power that writes the rules of the game, and protects the property rights of citizens and clients. The system has been capitalist without being laissez-faire: the dominant power provides the bulk of investment capital and a stable currency. It does not do this out of altruism, but because it profits from its position as the most advanced economy. It is dominant because it is able to outperform rivals in the leading sectors of the economy.

Unfortunately, the United States has been losing ground in all these leadership categories. Current trade and investment problems are symptoms of a deeper malaise. The downward trend started in the 1970's, but became more evident in the 1980's. Between 1972 and 1987, American manufacturing productivity increased only one-third as fast as West Germany and one-eighth as fast as Japan. During 1983-88, US fixed investments' share of GNP [Gross National Product] was one-half that of Japan. American growth since 1982 has depended primarily on increased labor participation; more workers rather than more productive workers. In the modern age, that is the antithesis of progress. Not only is this poor economics, it is harmful social policy and a dangerous national strategy.

As disturbing as this trend is, even more disturbing is the non-response of so many. To spend one's efforts trying to explain away or rationalize ominous developments rather than seek solutions is to become part of the problem. For when we cease to worry about the nation's relative standing in the world, the situation is truly lost.

William R. Hawkins is a contributor to Chronicles, *a conservative monthly journal of opinion.*

"Let's forget about the trade deficit. We have plenty of real deficits to worry about."

The Trade Deficit Is Not Serious

Herbert Stein and Warren Brookes

Editor's note: The following viewpoint is in two parts. Part I is by Herbert Stein. Part II is by Warren Brookes.

I

There seems to be a conspiracy against telling even the simplest truth.

This somber thought was brought home to me by an experience on a recent Tuesday afternoon. I'm goofing off, staying at home and watching daytime TV. I have a choice of 16 channels. On 15 of them beautiful women and handsome men are working out the complications of their love-lives, mostly in hospital rooms. I know that at my age I cannot expect any of these complications to be resolved during my lifetime, so I settle for C-SPAN and the U.S. Senate at "work."

I'm hearing a senator carrying on about how terrible it is that other countries insist on selling us more stuff than they buy from us. He demands that we let these countries know in no uncertain terms that we are not going to put up with that kind of thing any longer.

At first I am shocked. Is there no limit to what can be put out over the air, even in the daytime when children may be listening? But then I get over it and become more philosophical. I know that this senator has an undergraduate degree from one of our leading liberal arts colleges and another degree from one of our most eminent law schools. He is, however, a senator and may be forgiven for committing nonsense on the public airwaves.

But what about the trained staffs of international financial institutions who write serious reports about the need to correct "imbalances"—which is polite language for eliminating or reducing the U.S. trade deficit? What about the finance ministers from the

industrial countries who meet every six months or so to cook up plans for correcting these "imbalances"— again meaning the U.S. trade deficit? And what about my sophisticated economist friends who talk about the need to eliminate the trade deficit? What are they all talking about?

The More Candid Respond

I say to my economist friends that the trade deficit is not hurting the U.S., but, on the contrary, is helping us, and I ask them why we should be concerned about reducing the trade deficit. The more candid among them answer as follows: "We know that the trade deficit is not hurting us. But there are a lot of people out there—including presidents, senators, and congressmen—who think that the trade deficit is a bad thing and as long as it persists they will feel driven to protectionist measures, which would be very bad. In order to restrain the protectionist movement the trade deficit must be reduced."

What this comes down to is an argument for reducing the budget deficit as a way to reduce the trade deficit and thereby head off protectionism, even though we all know that the trade deficit is not hurting us and does not constitute a valid reason for protectionism.

Readers may know that I am more willing than most people to pay more taxes and give up some of my Social Security and Medicare benefits in order to balance the federal budget and run a surplus. There are good reasons for wanting to do that. But I would hate to pay anything in the hope of thereby heading off protectionism.

Some people have good reason to be protectionist; they have immediate interests at stake. No economist, however much devoted to free trade, ever denied that. These "knowing" protectionists will not be dissuaded by seeing the trade deficit disappear. But most people have no good reason to be protectionist. They support or tolerate protectionism out of ignorance. There should be a more efficient way to convert them to the virtues of free trade than by eliminating the trade deficit. Or, to put the case more modestly, it is worth trying to convert them by telling the truth. That is what economists are for. If some more "devious" ways of avoiding protectionism have to be found, let some one else do it.

Let's remember a few simple propositions.

1. The U.S. has a trade deficit because people in the rest of the world invest their savings here. This inflow of capital is voluntary on both sides—foreigners are seeking the best place to put their money and American governments and companies are seeking the best place to obtain money. Foreigners seeking to invest here have to obtain dollars. Their demand for dollars keep the exchange rate of the dollar at a level where U.S. imports exceed U.S. exports.

2. As a result of the capital inflow—and the accompanying trade deficit—since 1981, the stock of productive capital in the U.S. is now about $700 billion higher than it would otherwise have been. This fact is commonly misunderstood because people think the capital inflow is financing the budget deficit. It is true that foreigners have bought a large amount of U.S. Treasury securities. But if foreigners had not bought them they would have had to be bought by Americans, who would have had less of their own savings to invest in productive assets.

3. This inflow of capital has been mainly of benefit to American workers, who as a result of it work with a larger capital stock and have higher productivity and real incomes. It has also increased the U.S. tax base.

"I say to my economist friends that the trade deficit is not hurting the U.S., but, on the contrary, is helping us."

---

4. Large and persistent trade deficits have not prevented an unusually long recovery and the achievement of an unusually high level of total output.

5. Continuation of the capital inflow-trade deficit combination will increase the amount of interest and dividends that American governments and corporations have to pay to foreigners. But it will also increase the amount of capital in this country that would not otherwise be here, and that additional capital will generate the income to pay to foreigners. That income will not come out of income that Americans would otherwise have earned.

6. The inflow of capital and ownership of assets in the U.S. by foreigners is not a cause of dangerous dependence that is a political or security danger to us. What may be politically dangerous is the effort of governments to manipulate this relationship—an effort in which we are the leaders, unfortunately.

7. The inflow of goods and capital may not go on forever, but it is unlikely to stop so abruptly as to create difficulties for us. The two-sided inflow is an adaptation to basic conditions—propensities to save and investment opportunities, at home and abroad—that will change only gradually. The most serious qualification is that government efforts to manage exchange rates may cause such great uncertainties about the future of those rates that international capital flows dry up for a time.

Exchange Rates Everything

8. Protectionist measures imposed by government, ours and others, impair efficiency but do not cause the trade deficit. Trying to eliminate these measures would be worthwhile whether we have a deficit or a surplus, but success would not change the deficit.

9. Having a trade deficit is not a sign of low productivity or economic weakness. Poor, weak countries—like Brazil—can have trade surpluses. Rich, strong countries like us can have trade deficits. Everything depends on prices and exchange rates.

10. Let's forget about the trade deficit. We have plenty of real deficits to worry about—including the education deficit, the defense deficit, the poverty deficit and the investment deficit.

II

December 1989's noisy sale of Rockefeller Center to the Japanese has stirred up protectionist juices on Capitol Hill and further muddled some mercantilist minds in the Bush administration. In a global economy, ownership nationality is increasingly irrelevant.

Even so, total foreign investment in the United States is about 5 percent of U.S. gross national product, a fraction of U.S. investment shares in the economies of many of our biggest trading partners. The Japanese share of the U.S. commercial real estate base, even with the Rockettes, is well under 1 percent.

At least part of the hysteria is from the widely published perception by untrained observers such as author Susan Tolchin that "the United States is losing control over its own economic destiny."

That mercantilist absurdity is at least in part the result of dreadful U.S. Commerce Department data on both our capital and our trade flows. This inaccurate data vastly overstated our "deficits" in both areas and explains the dollar's persistent strength.

A Debtor Nation

In 1988, the United States was supposedly a "debtor nation"—to the tune of $536 billion. At today's interest rates, that would imply a net outflow of at least $40 billion to $50 billion in interest and dividend payments.

Instead, in 1988, we still earned about $2.2 billion more than we paid out in such payments. While this was sharply down from the $22 billion average of the previous three years, at least part of that drop was an exchange-rate anomaly.

The point is that our real "debtor position" is closer to $50 billion or less than 1 percent of gross national product. Pundits who worry about that kind of trivia have very little on their minds.

Unfortunately, the bad Commerce Department data has hyped this trivia into significance, and nowhere is this more evident than in the matter of the trade deficit.

Since 1986, this column has taken considerable scorn from Commerce officials for charging that their data overstated our trade deficit by as much as $20 billion to $30 billion.

But in June 1989, Commerce's Bureau of Economic Analysis implicitly admitted its error when it revised all of the 1986-1988 trade deficit data downward.

Net Export

In 1988, its original "Net Export" figure was $100.2 billion in constant 1982 dollars. Now, the revised number is $74.9 billion, a $25.3 billion cut. In 1987, the revision's reduction was $13.2 billion, and in 1986, the reduction was nearly $8 billion.

The main reason for these reductions is, as we charged, because U.S. exports in services (financial, legal, engineering construction, etc.) were drastically undercounted in the original data.

Harry Freeman of American Express pointed out in a *Wall Street Journal* article, "Nearly 10 years ago, representatives of the service sector companies worked out a plan with the Commerce Department to improve the data on service sector exports. Both groups believed that tens of billions of dollars of service exports. . . were not being counted as exports."

"Our actual trade deficit . . . was only $74 billion. In an economy of $4.926 trillion, that's a miniscule 1.5 percent and certainly no basis for a new orgy of U.S. trade chauvinism."

It has taken too long to make these adjustments. So far they have primarily been made to the 1988 data, which now show that our actual trade deficit (not the inflated merchandise deficit) was only $74 billion. In an economy of $4.926 trillion, that's a miniscule 1.5 percent and certainly no basis for a new orgy of U.S. trade chauvinism.

But that may explain why Democrats in Congress are now suddenly getting "cost-conscious" about the Commerce Department's data gathering and analysis and are deliberately undercutting the efforts to strengthen that process.

In October 1989, they cut the BEA's budget by $1.7 million and the Census Bureau's current budget by $16 million, and they also cut the budget for the 1990 decennial census by nearly $60 million.

Commerce Cuts

"These are very substantial cuts," said Michael Darby, undersecretary of Commerce and head of its economics division. "Not only will this wipe out our whole effort to improve the quality and accuracy of all of our data, from productivity to trade, but it will cut deeply into our current data reporting capacity."

Mr. Darby said in an interview, "If we can't maintain real statistical integrity, we are going to have to drop certain reports, because I will not tolerate the publication of substandard data."

These cutbacks come at a time when Congress wants a whole slew of detailed new reports from Commerce under the 1988 Omnibus Trade bill. If Congress were really interested in truth instead of political posturing, it would restore those millions to Commerce data efforts, and maybe we wouldn't need that Trade Bill anymore.

Herbert Stein is the former chairperson of the president's Council of Economic Advisers and is now a fellow at the American Enterprise Institute, a conservative organization in Washington, D.C. that analyzes political and economic affairs. Warren Brookes is a nationally syndicated columnist.

"Americans everywhere have become far more dependent upon—even addicted to—imports over the past few years."

Consumer Buying Habits Perpetuate the Trade Deficit

Art Pine

The once-depressed Rust Belt region around Cleveland is rebounding visibly these days, and Laura Rosenbaum and David Mortenson—a thirtysomething, two-income, white-collar couple—are back on a buying spree.

During the past 18 months, the comfortably heeled suburbanites have acquired a new car, an exercise machine, new bedroom furniture, a food processor, a computer, a briefcase and chic new eye frames—just to mention a few of the items.

But not everything they have bought will benefit the Cleveland area's resurging economy—or even that of the United States. The car is from West Germany, the food processor from France, the briefcase from Thailand and the glasses from Austria. Even the computer, ostensibly U.S.-made, contains components from Southeast Asia.

"I wouldn't have the foggiest idea where they were made, nor do I care," said Mortenson, who runs a chain of fast-food stores in the Cleveland area, drawing a nod of agreement from his wife. "We're really in the generation that's beyond worrying about that."

Addicted to Imports

The Cleveland-area couple aren't alone. Americans everywhere have become far more dependent upon—even addicted to—imports over the past few years.

David C. Lund, a Commerce Department economist, estimates that imports' share of what Americans buy has soared from 12.8% in 1970 to 22% today, with only scant indications of slowing. In dollar terms, import volume has doubled to a projected $475 billion in 1989 from $244 billion in 1982.

Imports actually bring some economic benefits. They can offer lower prices and higher quality for American consumers. Imports of capital goods—the equipment that American business uses for manufacturing—have been rising particularly sharply, and they should boost domestic production.

But over the years, competition from imports has also ravaged some industries.

Increased Imports

The current flood of overseas goods has defied the devaluation of the dollar since 1985, which has made imports more expensive compared to American-made goods. If the dollar had remained at its 1985 level, Japanese products would now be only half as expensive as they are.

And imports have continued to increase in volume despite the recent slowdown in U.S. economic growth, which might have dampened overall demand for both domestic and imported goods. Although the Commerce Department reported that imports fell a sharp 3.9% in September 1989, they had soared 5% the previous month, and analysts expect import levels to continue to rise more than they fall.

Alfred E. Eckes, a member of the U.S. International Trade Commission, which monitors the flow of trade, said import buying has "ratcheted up" to a new, seemingly immovable proportion. "We're in a new era," Eckes proclaimed.

"All the indications point to continuing competition even beyond what has occurred so far," said John K. Ryans, a Kent State University economist who advises several Ohio firms. "If people thought import competition was rough in the 1980s, wait until you see the 1990s."

Fortunately for the U.S. trade balance, exports have risen even faster than imports since 1987. But some analysts fear that exports will not be able to keep growing fast enough to prevent the trade deficit from edging back up.

Mototada Kikkawa of Columbia University's Center on Japanese Economy and Business warns that with

America's export capacity already strained to the hilt, the push to cut the trade deficit "has to bump up against the wall . . . as long as imports remain persistently high."

U.S. Trade

New forecasts by the Treasury Department predict that further improvement in the U.S. trade stance "is at best likely to be very modest" and "the possibility of deterioration . . . next year [1990] cannot be excluded."

Some economists find a silver lining in the import surge. David Richardson of the University of Wisconsin argues that consumers are benefiting from lower prices and, in many cases, better goods.

Imports are competing most heavily in old-line manufactured goods that "we should be pleased to be moving out of," Richardson contends. Import competition "has invited us to increase our skill level."

In the capital goods sector, imports now command 41% of the U.S. market, nearly double the 23% of 1982. These imports, Richardson points out, actually boost the U.S. economy's productive capacity.

"America's capital goods industries 'have been devastated' by import competition."

But critics of the trend point out that it also means a continued drain of traditional U.S. jobs—often with serious short-term economic pain in the affected industries.

America's capital goods industries "have been devastated" by import competition, complains Pat Choate, Washington-based vice president for policy analysis at TRW Inc. "We really have sacrificed a lot."

Columbia University's Kikkawa points out that imports of machinery and transportation equipment alone since the early 1980s have risen almost as much as the entire U.S. trade deficit. "Once, these were America's representative export industries," he noted.

Some analysts also fret that the United States has become so dependent upon imports that it would not be able to obtain important components—from machine tools and microchips to portions of fighter plane wings—in case of a war or even a limited conflict.

Depending on overseas suppliers "could sap the technological competition of U.S. weaponry" and "could disrupt the flow of materiel" to combat forces, warns a study by the Washington-based Center for Strategic and International Studies.

Consumer Goods

Imports' gains in the consumer goods field have been far more visible and, in some cases, even more devastating to domestic manufacturers.

Foreigners' share of the overall U.S. consumer goods market has held relatively steady, rising from 13.8% in 1982 to a peak of 16.3% in 1985 before slipping to 14.7% in 1989. But for some consumer products, import penetration has grown sharply. The market share for imports has tripled during the 1980s, for example, for toys, apparel and musical instruments.

Joseph Buzalewski, manager of Academy Music Co. in Cleveland Heights, has seen that phenomenon close up. His store provides instruments for the Cleveland Symphony and several local schools.

Until the 1960s, Buzalewski says, virtually all the band instruments that Academy carried were U.S.-made. Then Japan started making guitars—"junk at first, but gradually their quality improved." Later, Japan branched out into pianos, woodwinds and electronic keyboards.

Asian Imports

South Korea and Taiwan joined the bandwagon in the 1970s and 1980s, first with cheap guitars and, more recently, with quality instruments of other kinds. Now, even China is getting into the act. "It's a shame," Buzalewski says, "but that's the way it is."

Columbia University's Kikkawa cites a litany of reasons for the shift:

• The high value of the U.S. dollar in the early 1980s made imports far more competitive in price than they had been, providing sufficient profits to enable foreigners to set up the distribution centers and service networks needed to gain a strong foothold in the U.S. market.

• Partly because of the lack of competition earlier, many U.S. firms had become fat and lazy, burdened by high labor and materials costs and low productivity. In far too many cases, the quality of U.S. goods was low.

• At the same time, newly industrializing countries such as South Korea, Taiwan and Brazil were developing the ability to produce far more sophisticated goods, from quality steel components to autos, airplanes and even computers.

U.S. Firms Abroad

• U.S. firms, caught in a squeeze, began shopping overseas for cheaper materials and components. In some cases, they moved entire production lines to new plants abroad to take advantage of lower labor costs there.

• Deregulation also helped open new U.S. markets for foreign firms, particularly in consumer electronics. Throughout most of the 1970s, for example, only 2% of the nation's telephone equipment was made abroad. Today, after deregulation, it is up to 18%.

• Finally, the American economy grew far more rapidly than those of Europe and Japan during most of the early 1980s, turning the United States into a huge economic vacuum cleaner that sucked in imports from all over the world.

To be sure, at least some of the fierce competition from imports that American firms experienced in the early 1980s has abated somewhat—either because the dollar's decline has made imports too costly or because U.S. firms have improved their quality.

Joel D. Marx, a medical equipment distributor, recalled that "imports were all over" the U.S. market during the early 1980s but have retreated substantially since the dollar began falling in 1985. "The only thing they're competitive on now is rubber gloves," he said.

Sven Langmack, a kitchen equipment maker, said that since late 1985 his firm has "gotten back" most of the customers that it had lost earlier to imports. "We even sell to the Japanese," he said.

But studies under way by Washington economist Catherine L. Mann show that the impact of the declining dollar has been felt mostly by consumer goods. Imports of capital goods have continued virtually unabated.

Many buyers have found that kicking the import habit is not easy. Many of the most popular consumer electronics products— from radios to videocassette recorders—are not even made in the United States. And in many cases, brands with American names either are made overseas or contain major components that are manufactured abroad.

William Stokey, a spade-drill manufacturer in the nearby town of Dover, says his firm bought a piece of Pratt & Whitney machinery a few years ago specifically because it was an old-line American brand name, only to find that it was made in Japan.

Joseph Funnell, a trouble-shooter for the telephone company in Cleveland, finds the same problem with consumer purchases. "You may think something is American-made, but you're liable to find out that it's not," he says.

As a result of the experiences of the early 1980s, some U.S. manufacturers may have lost substantial numbers of customers to foreign suppliers for the long haul.

Donald Wright, a Cleveland-area machine shop owner, started buying Japanese-made machine tools in the early 1980s. The Japanese had begun to deliver their products within 10 days after they were ordered. By contrast, U.S. firms required a lead time of $2^1/2$ years.

Foreign Superiority

In May 1989, Wright bought an expensive new lathe, and he again picked a Japanese brand. "To be honest, we didn't even look at a U.S. supplier," he says. "When something works, you don't shop around to change."

As Kent State's Ryans points out, many American firms that either began buying overseas or moved their production facilities abroad during the high-dollar days of the early 1980s are unlikely to switch back soon. Such decisions, he says, "are long-term things."

Malachi Mixon III, who heads a firm in Elyria, Ohio, that makes medical equipment, says that 10 years ago he "didn't buy anything abroad" because he could get it all here—at the quality and price that he wanted.

"Imports' gains in the consumer goods field have been far more visible and, in some cases, even more devastating to domestic manufacturers."

But today, while he still prefers to buy from local suppliers, Mixon has a buyer "traveling all over the world"—to Colombia, Taiwan, China and Japan—to shop for lower-cost items because "it's necessary to help stay competitive."

Bringing about the policies to remedy this "will be far harder to accomplish than many analysts imagine," Kikkawa says.

Harald B. Malmgren, a Washington-based trade consultant, points out that the move by Japanese manufacturers to set up U.S. production facilities is beginning to cut into import sales in the United States.

But even in the Cleveland area, attitudes toward buying imports are changing.

"My father had this feeling that it was better to . . . buy American, but my impression being in Cleveland today is that people don't care anymore," Laura Rosenbaum said. "Those days are past."

Art Pine is a staff writer for the daily Los Angeles Times.

"The persistent trade deficit can also be linked to the practices of U.S. industrialists—as opposed to workers or consumers—in the 1980s."

viewpoint 14

Consumers Are Not Responsible for the Trade Deficit

Dollars & Sense

The trade deficit, that large splotch of red ink that won't go away, continues to dominate discussions of U.S. economic policy. Trade in tangible goods ("merchandise trade") was in deficit by $137 billion in 1988. (Imports of foreign goods exceeded exports of U.S. goods by that amount.) This was an improvement over 1987's record deficit of $170 billion, but in recent months the deficit has stopped shrinking.

The trade "problem," of course, is another policy issue that is subject to much political interpretation and definition. Conventional political wisdom holds that the trade deficit is a product of U.S. consumers who buy too many imported goods and U.S. workers whose high wages make U.S. goods uncompetitive in the world market. This "living beyond our means" interpretation leads logically to calls for "austerity" or belt-tightening on the part of consumers and workers, a refrain commonly heard in discussions of the trade deficit's twin—the federal budget deficit.

U.S. Trade Patterns

A closer look at the past 10 years of U.S. trade patterns paints a more complicated—if not altogether different—picture. For starters, the high-interest rate/strong dollar policies of the Volcker Federal Reserve Board and the Reagan administration in the early 1980s had much to do with the ballooning of the trade deficit. These policies made U.S. goods much more expensive in foreign markets, while lowering the prices of imported goods in the United States. At the same time, the demand for U.S. exports was hindered by slow growth in the world economy, especially Western Europe.

The persistent trade deficit can also be linked to the practices of U.S. industrialists—as opposed to workers or consumers—in the 1980s. U.S. corporations have been shifting production overseas to take advantage of cheaper foreign labor for quite some time. Offshore production adds to the trade deficit because it increases imports into the United States while decreasing exports. More recently, U.S. firms have fallen behind their foreign counterparts in many industries, thanks to out-dated production methods, top-heavy management structures, and an emphasis on short-term profits instead of long-term investment.

If misguided macroeconomic policies and flawed corporate strategies are behind the trade deficit, then austerity policies enforced on consumers and workers are unlikely to resolve U.S. trade problems in the long run.

Deficit Origins

Until 1971, the United States had not run a trade deficit in this century. The trade surplus was never particularly large, seldom reaching 1% of all goods and services sold in the economy. But it was a reassuring symbol of the strength of U.S. industry. When the red ink appeared in 1971, it was only $2 billion, a piddling 0.2% of GNP [gross national product]. But that first deficit symbolized something larger—intensified international competition for U.S. corporations and the inability of the U.S. government to orchestrate the world economy as thoroughly as it once did. . . .

By the mid-1980s, . . . most categories of domestically produced manufactured goods and machinery had begun losing ground to foreign competition. For example, metalworking machinery, a major component of the capital goods industry, had long been a leading export of the United States. After 1981, machinery exports slumped dramatically (almost 50% in two years); meanwhile, between 1980 and 1986 the value of imports in that category more than doubled.

Some U.S. goods retained their export edge, but ironically for an industrial power, these were primary products such as agricultural commodities and coal.

Dollars & Sense, "A Sea of Red Ink," April 1989. Reprinted with permission.

Yet even exports of agricultural products—a stronghold of the U.S. economy—fell by 50% between 1981 and 1986. Among the finished products that are emblematic of industrialized countries, commercial aircraft and chemicals were among the few in which the world continued to buy American.

The sudden, dramatic decline in the U.S. balance of trade in the early 1980s suggests equally dramatic causes. Two can be readily identified. The strong dollar during this period was a key factor. Between 1980 and its peak in early 1985, the dollar's value relative to other leading currencies jumped by 70%. That rise made U.S. goods much more expensive to foreigners and foreign goods cheaper to Americans.

Stagnation in Europe and many third world economies in the 1980s also aggravated the U.S. trade deficit. The economies of U.S. trading partners, except for Japan and Canada, grew even more slowly in the 1980s than did that of the United States. Between 1981 and 1987, average annual growth in GNP was 1.8% in Europe and 2.2% in "developing" countries. This compared to an annual growth rate of 2.7% in the United States. In the 1960s and 1970s, by contrast, European and third world economies grew more rapidly than the United States economy.

Consequently, U.S. exports grew more slowly than imports. Stagnation in other countries depressed the demand for U.S. goods by foreign consumers and businesses. In 1981, to cite just one example, U.S. producers sold $2.1 billion worth of metalworking machinery abroad, their peak year for exports. In the very next year, as recession hit foreign economies, U.S. exports fell by nearly $550 million, a drop they had not recovered from by 1986. Imports of metalworking machinery, which stood at $1.6 billion in 1981, had jumped to $2 billion by 1984. As the U.S. economy grew out of its recession in 1982, these imports grew as well and by 1986 reached $3.2 billion.

Dollar Drop

By mid-1985, it became clear to both the Reagan administration and the governments of the other major capitalist economies that the strong dollar was inflicting too much damage on U.S. manufacturers, raising the risk of a recession in the United States and much of the world. The "Group of Seven" nations agreed in September of that year to drive the dollar down, and in the next year and a half, it fell by some 50% against both the German mark and the Japanese yen.

Eventually, the drop in the dollar did help boost U.S. exports. In 1988, U.S. exports jumped by nearly 27% compared with an 8% increase in imports. This export boom shaved some $33 billion off the trade deficit in 1988. Much of this improvement came from a reduction in the U.S. trade deficit with the nations of the European Community, which fell by a startling 47%, to $17 billion from $30 billion in 1987. The deficit with Japan dropped by a less impressive 7%, to $55 billion. The U.S. trade deficit with the newly industrialized countries of Asia fell by about 15%, from nearly $38 billion in 1987 to $32 billion in 1988.

It seems unlikely, however, that the U.S. economy can continue to export its way out of the trade deficit. In the last three months of 1988, export growth was flat. The economies of U.S. trading partners in Europe and much of the third world remain sluggish. And rising domestic interest rates will also put upward pressure on the dollar once again.

"The behavior of U.S. corporations and their foreign competitors since the dollar's drop also suggests that the trade deficit is unlikely to disappear quickly or easily."

The behavior of U.S. corporations and their foreign competitors since the dollar's drop also suggests that the trade deficit is unlikely to disappear quickly or easily. Many foreign manufacturers have held the line on product prices despite the increase in the value of the dollar, which should make foreign goods more expensive in the United States. Thus, since the dollar's peak in early 1985, import prices have risen only 30%, despite a 70% increase in foreign currency values. In effect, many importers, especially Japanese manufacturers, have been willing to sacrifice profits in the short run to hold onto their markets in the United States.

At the same time, some U.S. exporters have taken advantage of the dollar's fall to increase their short-term profits. Instead of using the currency-induced decline in the prices of U.S. exports to expand their sales, many U.S. manufacturers have raised the prices of their exports to boost profits.

U.S. export strength is also constrained by the decisions of many U.S. manufacturers in the 1980s to abandon or shun production of a range of consumer goods—from cameras to VCRs. Such decisions affect more than U.S. exports—U.S. consumers have no choice but to rely on imports for many product purchases.

It seems that continued sharp declines in the trade gap are not in the cards. The dollar has stopped falling, and it's not clear that further drops in the currency would improve the situation in any case, given the responses of both U.S. and foreign firms. Without a major departure in U.S. corporate and government policy, the trade deficit will remain a large splotch of red ink.

Dollars & Sense *is a monthly socialist magazine.*

Regional Trading Blocs Will Harm the U.S.

Edwin A. Finn Jr.

Unless something can be done to stop it, international trade will soon have degenerated from relatively free exchange to a system of three separate trading blocs. This is not just a threat. It is an emerging reality.

Since 1987, the broad outlines of these blocs have started to emerge. Call them the United States of North America, the United States of Europe and the United States of Asia. Statistics show that trade inside these blocs is growing at a rapid pace, while trade among these blocs is either declining or growing far more moderately. This reverses decades of booming and beneficial trade among the continents.

The trend is most pronounced in Europe, where regional integration is most advanced. Inside the European Economic Community, trade jumped nearly 15% since 1985, while EEC trade with nonmember countries actually fell by an estimated 10%.

Trade Patterns

In 1988 the trend surfaced in North America, with trade among the U.S., Canada and Mexico growing almost 20% in the first nine months, compared with a 5% increase in North America's trade with Europe. These trade patterns are expected to intensify as the Canada-U.S. Free Trade Agreement and the European community's 1992 unification plans take full effect.

Japan, meanwhile, has virtually recolonized Asia, building factories throughout the region. Little wonder Japan's trade with its Asian neighbors jumped an estimated 30% in 1988. Overall, trade within a nine-nation Asian bloc defined by *Forbes* grew at a 32% pace in 1988's first nine months. Asian trade with Europe and with North America in the same period was up substantially, too—10% and 17%, respectively—but not nearly as robustly as intra-Asian trade.

What accounts for the new trade patterns? To a

great degree, protectionism, and the U.S. itself is no starry-eyed exception. Despite the Reagan Administration's commitment to free trade, protectionist actions in Washington since 1981 have pushed the U.S.'s share of total imports subject to quota or official restraint from 12% up to 23%. So-called "managed trade agreements" have been enacted to restrict imports of autos, machine tools, carbon steel and semiconductors. On top of that, the U.S. has imposed higher tariffs on motorcycles, specialty steel and shingles and shakes.

Congress is talking about setting up its own trade office to keep an eye on the presidentially appointed U.S. Trade Representative. Such an office would work in much the same way the Congressional Budget Office squares off against the President's Office of Management & Budget. This approach appears to be another example of congressional usurpation of presidential powers, encouraged by seemingly perennial Republican possession of the White House and Democratic control of Congress. But it could encourage protectionism, since Congress tends to represent parochial interests, while the White House tends to represent the interests of the country as a whole.

Competing Successfully

Even America's academic community—long a standard-bearer for free trade—is beginning to warm to selective forms of protectionism. One group of academics advances the argument that trade advantages in the late 20th century are increasingly determined not so much by a country's natural resource base or the skills of its people as by public policy: taxation, education and business regulation. In other words, government plays the major role in determining whether a country's businesses will be able to compete successfully with their foreign rivals.

The U.S. must fight fire with fire, these academics argue. For the U.S. to compete with Europe and Asia,

Edwin A. Finn Jr., "Sons of Smoot-Hawley." Reprinted by permission of *Forbes* magazine, February 6, 1989. © Forbes Inc., 1989.

Washington should help private American companies by funding research in selected sectors such as semiconductors and high-definition television.

If the U.S. is hardly innocent, it is not the worst offender. Protectionism is rampant in some European countries. Italy has adopted regulations that all but ban Japanese cars from the Italian market. France now routinely holds Japanese electronics products at the border indefinitely for small infractions.

Despite the European Economic Community's protestations that the 1992 accord will promote free trade worldwide, the Community's own projections show that trade inside the EEC is expected to grow 10% in the next six to ten years, while the Community's imports from non-EEC countries will grow only 2% to 3%.

Protectionist Trends

Business people are well aware of the trend toward protectionism and are acting in what they see as their own best interests. To ensure their access to foreign markets, they are increasingly setting up plants inside those markets. Thus, Korea's Hyundai Motor Co. has set up a plant in Canada to make its Sonata midsize cars for customers in Canada and the U.S. Foreign textile manufacturers from Hong Kong and elsewhere are setting up shop in the Caribbean, largely because President Reagan's Caribbean Basin Initiative assures these islands preferential access to the U.S. consumer market.

Industry experts say that IBM, worried that Europe's 1992 regulations could exclude it completely from the continent's data processing business, is considering joint ventures with European firms.

"Despite the European Economic Community's protestations that the 1992 accord will promote free trade worldwide, . . . the Community's imports from non-EEC countries will grow only 2% to 3%."

Smaller U.S. companies, fearing a protectionist backlash, are scrambling to get inside Europe well before 1992. Thus, Richardson Electronics, Ltd., a LaFox, Ill. manufacturer (sales, $120 million), recently acquired its first European factory, in Brive, France. Says Edward Richardson, the company's chairman and CEO [chief executive officer], "We feel it would be much better to be in place when it all happens than to try to get in after 1992."

Will someone cry halt to the protectionist trend before it escalates into a trade war? It's impossible to say, but if a trade war does erupt, each of the three blocs is in an excellent position to go it alone.

Why? Because each bloc is roughly similar in macroeconomic terms. Each has solid sources of capital and technology. Each has considerable natural resources, though not quite enough to be self-sufficient. Each has regions where an abundant supply of inexpensive labor is readily available—North America in Mexico, Europe in Spain and Portugal, Asia in Indonesia, Thailand and the Philippines.

Europe, cocky over the prospects of 1992, is clearly in the mood to listen to protectionist arguments. The U.S., worried over its relative industrial decline, is too. Perhaps the most vulnerable bloc is Asia, where the consumer market, at 480 million people, isn't as developed as in either the U.S. or Europe. Many Asians, remembering World War II, fear Japanese hegemony over their region. Also, Asia isn't knit together by a union such as the Canada-U.S. Free Trade Agreement or the European Economic Community.

But Asia's growing trade ties could prove a surprisingly powerful incentive to form some sort of union. Says David Hale of Kemper Financial Services Inc., a leading expert on international trade patterns, "Adding a political structure is just a short step from what the Asian trading market has [already] done."

Modified Protectionism

Even those who support some form of modified protectionism agree that once the trend starts, it is difficult to reverse. Industrial policy could degenerate from the protection of selected industries to a restrictionist orgy benefiting companies and groups for political reasons, not only in the U.S. but everywhere.

After half a century of relative harmony on the trade front, protectionism is clearly making a noticeable comeback. Believers in free trade will make a big mistake if they treat the threat lightly.

Edwin A. Finn Jr. is a senior editor at Forbes, *a weekly economics magazine.*

"A trading bloc . . . expands the reach of free trade, but within an area in which it is possible to have a common macroeconomic strategy."

Regional Trading Blocs Will Benefit the U.S.

Robert Kuttner

On January 1, 1989, after bitter debate in Canada, the Free Trade Agreement took effect, creating generally open commerce between the United States and Canada. Bush administration officials have hinted that Mexico might next be welcomed into a North American common market. Across the Atlantic, the 12-nation European Community is working feverishly toward the 1992 deadline for completion of a free single market. In the Orient, Japan is becoming the mother country of a latter-day Greater East Asia Coprosperity Sphere, linked not by the Imperial Navy, but by selectively low trade barriers, Japanese bank credits, foreign aid, Japanese investment, joint ventures, and the power of the yen.

On the face of it, these developments seem cause for celebration. Both the U.S.-Canada deal and post-1992 Europe can be expected to create more free trade, and even the Asian economic sphere has its efficiencies. Still, most economists and U.S. diplomats are wary about the prospect of a world economy that consists of a few large trading blocs.

Free traders argue that even if a trading bloc doesn't raise new, collective barriers to trade with the outside world, it can be destructive both of economic efficiency and of the political logic of the trading system. Whenever one nation's products are favored over another's, this is in some sense a loss for economic efficiency and consumer choice. However much it expands U.S.-Canada trade, a North American free trade area means that U.S. consumers have freer access to Canadian products than to, say, Korean ones.

To put the matter in political terms, champions of free trade worry that any retreat into bilateral deals undermines the General Agreement on Tariffs and Trade, the GATT, whose most sacred principle is that the products of all nations should get the same

Robert Kuttner, "Bloc That Trade," *The New Republic,* April 17, 1989. Reprinted by permission of THE NEW REPUBLIC, © 1989, The New Republic, Inc.

treatment as the "most favored nation." A favorite metaphor (and tired cliché) of free traders is the bicycle. You have to keep pedaling faster or you wobble. Ever freer trade is said to be necessary to keep the multilateral system from backsliding into protectionism. Hence the fear that regional free trade is the first slide down a slippery slope, away from postwar multilateralism, toward inward-looking economic fortresses reminiscent of the depressed 1930s.

Trading Blocs

In trying to decide whether these fears are valid, it helps to locate trading blocs in their historical context. The late 1980s have seen the crumbling of the world economic system conceived in the 1940s, though the institutional shell of that system endures. The creations of the great burst of postwar statecraft—the GATT, the World Bank, the International Monetary Fund—reflected America's determination to build an international economic system that would avoid repeating two errors: the excesses of laissez-faire during the 1920s, which helped trigger the Great Depression; and the protectionist response of many nations during the early 1930s, which only deepened it.

These were essentially opposite impulses—one toward more planning and government control, and one toward less. They were reconciled in a global economic regime that steered a midcourse between John Maynard Keynes and Adam Smith. In the grand postwar compromise, free trade presumably reigned internationally, while domestic market forces were tempered by Keynesian macroeconomic stabilization, trade unionism, and a welfare state. In practice, free commerce across national borders was also limited by fixed exchange rates, capital controls, the dominance of the U.S. dollar, and relatively high tariffs. Still, the stated goal of the global trading system was a gradual and relentless move toward ever freer trade.

Recent political and economic shifts have undermined the logic of this U.S.-anchored postwar economic system. For one, the bipolarity of the early cold war is softening, undermining the geo-political logic of membership in a U.S.-led system. At the same time, a relatively weakened United States is no longer able to serve as the flywheel of the world economy. But more than that, the newly liberalized and integrated global economy has outrun the domestic stabilizers that were supposed to give each nation a measure of control over its economic destiny. Now that goods, services, and money flow so freely in and out of the U.S. economy, for example, traditional forms of government control—fiscal and monetary policy—have less impact than they once did. Similarly, it is harder these days for a government to enforce a generous social policy—a high minimum wage, say—without losing markets to lower-wage competition.

"Recent history offers a frantic oscillation between the sacred ideological imperative of ever freer markets and the profane business of looking with almost equal urgency for practical economic stabilizing devices."

The appeal of a trading bloc, even for a free trade purist, is that it expands the reach of free trade, but within an area in which it is possible to have a common macroeconomic strategy, and a common understanding of desirable social arrangements. This is, of course, not possible when the free trade area is the entire world, and the reach of the market overwhelms the reach of the polity. In that sense the vogue of free trade areas suggests an urge to restore the compromise between laissez-faire and government regulation that was the aim of postwar reforms.

Laissez-Faire and Planning

But this is seldom acknowledged. In the revisionist collective memory of the 1940s, postwar reconstruction is celebrated for its economic liberalism, not for its careful mix of laissez-faire and planning. The stabilization lessons of the 1930s and 1940s have been all but forgotten, and the very concept has been banished from the economic lexicon. The only practical choice is seen as ever freer markets, which are presumed inherently virtuous, versus "protectionism," which is by definition self-serving and vicious. Recent history offers a frantic oscillation between the sacred ideological imperative of ever freer markets and the profane business of looking with almost equal urgency for practical economic stabilizing devices to offset the chaos that

laissez-faire can engender. Viewed in that light, the attractions of a free trade area are obvious. It allows one to have his cake and eat it too. It expands freer trade, but in a manageable context.

Superb Compromise

In Western Europe, the champions of the common market have always been the relative economic liberals. They understood that creation of a pan-European market would wean individual nations from nationalist and statist economics. The early opponents of European integration were socialists who feared that the unleashing of market forces would wreck their economic planning. Yet even Europe's liberals appreciated that pure laissez-faire was untenable. In their conception, a transnational common market was a superb compromise between market and state.

This same synthesis can be seen in the texture of the U.S.-Canada deal. It is mainly an agreement to phase out tariffs and "non-tariff barriers," such as quotas, technical standards, and regulatory obstacles, over a ten-year period. It ducks some key questions, such as the legitimacy of subsidies, and papers over several others. The deal also assents to some major sectors of managed trade, such as lumber and automobile parts, which account for a sizable share of cross-border commerce. Canadian auto parts are admitted duty-free to the United States but only if they are at least 50 percent made-in-Canada. This gives Canadian suppliers preference in the U.S. market, and slows down penetration by third-country suppliers, notably Japan.

The U.S. government has tried to paint the Canada deal as both a friend of free trade and a second-best alternative to it. While celebrating the deal as a victory for the forces of free trade, Secretary of State James Baker has warned other nations, virtually in the same breath, that if progress in the current Uruguay round of multilateral trade talks fails, the U.S.-Canada pact suggests a rough model of how the United States might choose to go it alone. The State Department has also claimed that the U.S.-Canada deal is really GATT-friendly, since other nations might join it. But that's silly. The relationship between the United States and Canada is in so many ways unique—the geographic proximity, comparable wage rates, extensive cross-border investment—that other nations won't be able to join in by merely signing on the dotted line. Also highly improbable is the much-discussed grand U.S.-Japan free trade area. Since most of Japan's trade barriers are covert, bargaining away the remaining overt barriers to U.S.-Japan trade would only worsen our bilateral trade deficit. Besides, a U.S.-Japan trade deal would be a virtual declaration of economic war on the European Community (which, incidentally, is also not likely to expand easily to encompass many other nations).

The differences between the U.S.-Canada deal and the post-1992 version of the European Community are significant. U.S.-Canada is merely a reciprocal agreement to reduce trade barriers. It is not a customs union, and does not establish a common external tariff. Nor does U.S.-Canada set up a supranational authority with real political power, like the EC Commission. To the extent that the U.S.-Canada Free Trade Area impinges on Canadian sovereignty, it cedes political sovereignty to market forces. The EC, in sharp contrast, doesn't cede sovereignty to the market so much as elevate sovereignty to a supranational body—and one that happens to believe in industrial policies, trade unionism, a welfare state, and the other elements of a 1940s-style mixed economy.

This explains much of the nervousness on this side of the Atlantic about Europe after 1992. American free traders have always viewed Brussels, headquarters of the EC, as a nest of closet mercantilists, and there is great suspicion that, as one former U.S. Treasury official recently wrote, "We may have created a Frankenstein that will regulate, not liberate, the European economy." Europe, to a far greater extent than the United States, has used national industrial policies, subsidies, technical standards, and deliberate policies of exclusion (mainly directed against the Japanese) to assure that the next generation of Euro-industry is around to compete in such key industries as semiconductors, aviation, consumer electronics, steel, and so on—and to create economic space in which to practice an advanced welfare state. In the shift to Community-wide standards as part of the 1992 "single market," these subsidies, quotas, technical regulations, etc., become Europeanized, not dismantled. That 1992 is the brainchild of Jacques Delors, a Frenchman and a socialist, only fuels American suspicions.

"The trading system may at last be recognizing that there are worse things than a dose of stability, and better fates than unadulterated laissez-faire."

The surprising success of the European Monetary System—a quite illiberal, decade-old mini-Bretton Woods zone of exchange rate stability anchored by the deutsche mark and the West German Bundesbank—also makes Washington uneasy. It suggests a monetary zone independent of the U.S. dollar. Indeed, the original, and most extreme, trading bloc of this century was the creation of Hitler's economics minister, Hjalmar Schacht, who used bilateral trade deals within a Reichmark area as a deliberate adjunct of Nazi foreign policy in the Balkans and in South America, where the Germans offered their trading partners a form of scrip exchangeable only for German products.

The Japanese have been far more nimble at paying obeisance to American norms of global openness while quietly pursuing their own regional course. By the visible indicators of tariffs or quotas, the Japanese economy appears open. There is no evidence of a "yen bloc," or of exclusionary bilateral Japanese treaties. Yet Japanese multinational firms tend to be rather more nationalistic than their American counterparts. There are growing linkages between Japanese firms and satellite industries in low-wage Asian countries. Japan has also become the world's No. 1 donor of foreign economic aid, much of which is closely linked to Japanese commercial objectives.

A Global Economy

Despite all these trends, one would be very hard-pressed to make a case that the world is really deteriorating into hard trading blocs. The interpenetration of the American, European, and Japanese economies by firms and banks flying various flags (and sometimes no flag—or several) suggests that a truly global economy is alive and well, despite the failure of a great deal of global trade to conform to GATT rules. Thus, when Honda, responding to "voluntary" restraints on American imports of Japanese cars, sets up shop in the United States, the ends of free international trade are being served. To the extent that the success of Japanese factories is due to management technique or manufacturing technology, Japan's comparative advantage is substantially realized even when Honda's factories are in the United States. One can imagine trading blocs, with strong barriers to capital flow and technology, that would impede such movement of technology, but today's relatively soft trading blocs pose no such barriers.

All of this suggests that the trading system may at last be recognizing that there are worse things than a dose of stability, and better fates than unadulterated laissez-faire. One can imagine several scenarios for the coming decades. At one extreme, the United States tries to maintain an idealized global free trade system, which it no longer has the power either to enforce or to anchor. At the other extreme, the world really does become three trading blocs, in which the EC survives as a semifortress, energized by new commercial links to a more liberal Eastern Europe; Japan realizes its ancient dream of regional dominion in partnership with the mercantilist ministates of the Pacific basin; and the United States is left with Canada and, by default, with the high-debt, low-enterprise hardship cases of the Third World—Brazil, India, Mexico, and assorted smaller economies, mainly in Latin America.

But a far more probable and benign scenario is that the United States will at last recognize two realities. First, it could admit that other nations need to take greater responsibility for the health of the trading system, both to uphold that system and to allow the

United States room to pursue its national economic self-interest. Freed of the burden of being the world's free trade role model, we could then be a tougher bargainer in bilateral negotiations and could prevail upon nations such as Germany and Japan to quit running chronic, huge trade surpluses. Second, the United States could recognize that few nations share our own view of the virtues of pristine laissez-faire. A more genuinely multilateral system would allow for various departures from purist free trade, ranging from national industrial policies, to technology and market-sharing deals, to the continued proliferation of regional blocs that introduce more liberalism to trade, even if they fall short of the global ideal.

Protectionist Measures

Lately there have been several noteworthy cracks in the purist dike, both in practice and in theory. Even the Reagan administration committed industrial policy, in ventures like Sematech. And trade reciprocity—tough bargaining for bilateral liberalizing of trade, even including the threat of punitive protectionist measures—is gaining respectability as a U.S. policy goal. The Bush administration, at this writing, is wrestling with the recognition that it matters whether the U.S. government helps the Japanese to gain a technological foothold in commercial aviation. And the coming of Europe 1992 will force the administration to clarify further its industrial goals—to ask, for example, whether the United States should mount a challenge to the United European attempt to set the standard for (and then dominating the manufacturing of) high-definition TV.

"A mixed system, under plural guardianship, could be a plus both for global stability and for the U.S. economy."

Perhaps, in this new context, the United States can begin devoting its energies toward negotiating common ground rules for a necessarily mixed system, rather than spending all its diplomatic capital in a vain attempt to preserve the purity of laissez-faire. A mixed system, under plural guardianship, could be a plus both for global stability and for the U.S. economy. It's time for the angel of the postwar system to look homeward.

Robert Kuttner is economics editor for The New Republic, *a weekly journal of opinion.*

A Unified Europe Will Promote U.S. Interests

Eugene J. McAllister

There is a tremendous amount of interest in the United States about 1992—the target date for completing the single market exercise. And that interest is well placed; 1992 is important for all of us, from the large U.S. multinational corporation with a European subsidiary to the relatively small U.S. manufacturer who may someday seek to export to Europe. Nineteen-ninety-two is also important to the man on the street because the single market effort will change Europe, and that will, of course, affect the United States. We in the government believe the single market, if successful—and by that I mean open—will be good for the United States. But the U.S. Government is not just hoping that the single market will be open, we are working hard to do everything within our power to assure that the single market will be open.

Let me outline how the U.S. Government looks at 1992.

First, the United States unequivocally supports European economic integration. In fact, this has been an underlying principle of U.S. foreign policy since World War II. The wisdom of this approach has been proven and is being proven. A united Europe, a purposeful Europe, is critical to addressing the Soviet threat. We can see that in nuclear arms negotiations, in efforts to restrict Soviet access to dual-use technologies, and in responding to regional issues or conflict. Economic integration—as manifested through the European Community—is one of the elements that draws Europe closer.

Second, in our view, 1992 is primarily a deregulatory exercise—we accept at face value the Economic Community's statements that they are trying to build a more economically efficient community, and we do not see a more economically efficient European Community as a threat. Rather, we

see it as good for the United States and the world. The European Community will become: a better market for U.S. products; a competitor that helps drive U.S. enterprises to excellence; and we believe that the efficiency gains that the EC achieves will, in one form or another, be available to the rest of the world.

Third, while we are optimistic about 1992, we are also wary about 1992. The value of 1992 to the rest of the world is that it is open—a single EC market will be larger than the U.S. market: 320 million people with a gross national product of $4.1 trillion. Our wariness is that the single market will be less than open, either as a result of discriminatory directives or regulations, narrow application of existing trade regulations, or through the failure of the Uruguay Round GATT [General Agreement on Tariffs and Trade] negotiations to develop worldwide rules for new areas, such as financial services.

Finally, in my view, we are entering a new period in international economic relations. The postwar policies must evolve to adapt to the economic, political, and social changes that are occurring in the world: the U.S. trade act; the debt crisis; the recognition on the part of the less developed nations that openness and an outward orientation are the keys to success. Nineteen-ninety-two can be one of the foundations for the future, and the European Community will help shape that future. Let me elaborate on each of these points.

European Economic Integration

The benefits of economic integration are recognized by a great many countries.

• The United States implemented a historic Free Trade Agreement with Canada—an agreement that goes beyond traditional trade agreements to cover investment, intellectual property, and services;

• Australia and New Zealand are pursuing what they call "closer economic relations";

• The six member states of the Association of South

Eugene J. McAllister, "U.S. Views on the EC Single Market Exercise," a speech delivered before the American Association of Exporters and Importers in New York City, May 18, 1989.

East Asian Nations have joined together in an attempt to create a common market; and

• There is another economic organization in Europe, the European Free Trade Association—Sweden, Switzerland, Austria, Norway, Finland, and Iceland—which was formed partly as a response to the creation of the European Community.

Benefits of Integration

But the champion of economic integration is the European Community. Since the Treaty of Rome was signed in 1957, the European Community has expanded from 6 to 9 to 10 to 12. The desire of nations to join the European Community is prima facie evidence of the benefits of integration. But let me offer some additional evidence.

• During the 10-year period in which EC tariffs were eliminated (1959 to 1969), intra-EC trade rose by 347%; by contrast, trade in the rest of the world rose only 130%.

• In specific cases, the benefits are clear as well. The year after Spain and Portugal joined the European Community, their trade with EC members rose over 40%. In fact, their bilateral trade shot up even more—over 79%. Economic growth accelerated from 2.7% to 5% a year in Spain and from 3.7% to 4.2% in Portugal, while unemployment rates are showing a definite downward trend.

• For Ireland, joining the European Community has resulted in payments from the common agricultural policy and regional assistance amounting to as much as 5% of GDP [gross domestic product].

• During the first 10 years of Britain's membership in the European Community, Britain's trade with EC member states rose 26% per year, in contrast to its trade with the rest of the world, which increased only 19% per year.

The United States has always supported the economic integration of Europe. Our reasoning is simple: An economically integrated Europe promotes political and social integration, and a united Europe—a strong Europe—is a cornerstone of U.S. foreign policy.

"An economically integrated Europe promotes political and social integration, and a united Europe—a strong Europe— is a cornerstone of U.S. foreign policy."

I have talked about the importance of 1992 as a continuation of a postwar political trend. Let me talk about 1992 as a purely economic venture.

For a number of years, we have talked about "Eurosclerosis"—that hardening of the economic arteries in the 1970s and 1980s that seemed to indicate that the EC nations were entering their twilight years. And there is a strong case that the EC nations have become burdened with the weight of too much regulation and have paid too little attention to the importance of dynamics and change. Economic statistics illustrate a discouraging loss of momentum in Europe.

• Real GDP growth slowed from a brisk 5% per year in the 1960s to a tortoise-like 1.2% in the first-half of the 1980s.

• Growth in the early 1980s was half what it was in the 1970s, despite the easing of the oil crisis.

• Unemployment has jumped from an average of 2% to 12% over the same timespan.

• Even today, with the 1992 program starting to put new life into the European economy, unemployment hovers around 10%-12% as compared to roughly 5% in the United States. As the U.S. economy is creating jobs at an unprecedented rate during the 1980s, total employment in the European Community has grown only anemically; indeed, in the early 1980s total employment in the European Community actually fell, according to EC Commission statistics.

Eurosclerosis

Clearly one factor contributing to "Eurosclerosis" has been the barriers to trade, the delays, distortions, technical costs, and duplication of effort. Let me offer some examples.

• The cost of customs formalities alone is reckoned to be nearly 2% of all intra-EC trade, which itself accounts for 14% of EC gross domestic product.

• Trucks running empty because of transport restrictions added 5% to the cost of transporting goods within the European Community in 1988.

• Technical barriers, such as automobile standards that require manufacturers to produce multiple variations on the same model, or drug regulations that oblige manufacturers to requalify drugs for 12 different countries, are very costly to European business.

Nineteen-ninety-two is motivated by the desire on the part of the EC nations to become more competitive—to reduce the drag on their economies created by unnecessary standards, inspections, customs requirements, and regulations. Because the single market is driven by this desire to become more competitive, I believe that there is a predisposition that 1992 will be outward oriented and open.

Some have suggested that the only thing worse than the failure of 1992 would be its success—that if 1992 is successful, we will be facing a much stronger economic competitor; a competitor that will sell more products in the United States and more aggressively challenge U.S. exports to third-country markets. This kind of reasoning is just plain wrong. Trade and growth are not a zero-sum game. A more vibrant and productive European Community is good for the United States, for Canada and Japan, and for the entire world.

I would also stress that a successful single market

initiative has potentially important and beneficial effects for the less developed countries (LDCs):

• A more integrated European Community could help catalyze LDC development by encouraging trade.

• Currently, the European Community absorbs a relatively small proportion of manufacturers from LDCs.

• The single market can redress this imbalance, and the European Community can share more of the responsibility of stimulating LDC growth.

Concerns About 1992

As I have pointed out, the United States is supportive, indeed, enthusiastic about EC integration—both from a foreign policy and economic perspective. But there is a caveat: The promise of 1992 will only be fulfilled if the European Community becomes more open, more outward oriented.

The need for the EC nations to remain competitive is the force driving 1992 and driving it in the direction of openness. But there are temptations.

The first is the difficulty of reversing years of social restraints on economic activity. Rapid change—the kind of change that affects jobs and personal financial security—will create pressures for exceptions, tradeoffs, or protection. How will the European Community respond?

The second temptation is the desire on the part of some to use the 1992 exercise as leverage to open foreign markets or to keep out those whose markets are not open—or perceived to be not open. Understandable, but difficult to achieve in a GATT consistent manner. Requiring trading partners to "pay or earn" their way into the EC market would be a very dangerous route for the European Community to follow.

The U.S. Government has been closely watching the 1992 initiative, and we have been sharing our concerns with the Commission and the governments of the member states. We have four types of concerns.

U.S. Concerns

First, we are concerned about attempts to apply to foreign investors or exporters the notion of "reciprocity," equivalent access, or other euphemisms that move us away from the principle of national treatment. In the second banking directive, the Commission initially called for reciprocity as a standard for foreign entry. Because the United States has domestic restrictions on interstate banking and banks underwriting securities, a strict interpretation of reciprocity could keep U.S. banks out of Europe. We prefer the principle of national treatment. A bank from the European Community operating in the United States would be treated the same as a U.S. bank in similar circumstances and vice versa. The standard of national treatment is fair, predictable, and open. We are encouraged to see that, thanks in part to the Administration's rapid and forceful reaction to

this idea, the Commission has revised the directive to define reciprocity as national treatment plus "effective market access." EC representatives suggest that this means that national treatment must apply not only on paper but also in terms of actual opportunity for EC banks to participate fully in the market—free of hidden or bureaucratic barriers. The Commission's revision is a step in the right direction. However, we must continue to watch this issue closely.

A *second* issue of concern to the United States is recent EC actions on "rule of origin"—those rules or regulations that are used to define the "nationality" of a product in dumping cases, where higher tariffs are imposed on a product from a certain country. Restrictive rules of origin have the potential to harm U.S. export interests, divert trade from third countries to the EC market, or induce investment in the European Community on noncommercial grounds. We are concerned by two recent decisions—with regard to Ricoh copiers and semiconductor chips—that illustrate the potential for decisions to affect business and commercial decisions, such as where to locate manufacturing facilities and research and development operations. We are looking very closely at the possible interaction of rules of origins and other trade measures, such as quotas, that might create a systemic bias in favor of locating in Europe, rather than exporting to Europe.

"The United States is supportive, indeed, enthusiastic about EC integration—both from a foreign policy and economic perspective."

Third, we are concerned about quotas or local content requirements. Many of the EC countries have national trade barriers, such as quotas on automobile imports. Will these national quotas be translated into EC-wide quotas? The Nissan Bluebird automobile manufactured in Britain, apparently, will be allowed to enter France unhindered by the French quota on Japanese cars. But is this a one-time exception based on some local content requirement? The Honda plant in Marysville, Ohio, may be interested in exporting cars to Europe. How will our Hondas be treated in France, Italy, and the entire European Community? We are also disturbed by internal measures that can serve as nontariff barriers. A good example of this type of measure is the proposed broadcasting directive, which stipulates that a majority of programming on EC broadcasting networks be of EC origin. Such restrictions could potentially restrict our access to a market in which we have been phenomenally successful.

Fourth, one of the most critical elements of 1992 will be the standards, certification, and testing processes. There is potential for discrimination here. EC-wide standards may bar differing U.S. technologies; lack of transparency may prevent effective U.S. input or shorten lead time for U.S. exporters to make design changes before new rules go into effect; U.S. producers and testing bodies may not get equal access to an EC-wide testing and certification system. We are now awaiting a public EC draft proposal on a new "global approach" to standards, testing, and certification which may clarify some of these issues. However, our bottom line in this critical area is transparency; we want the opportunity to comment on the standards, certification, and testing procedures before they are implemented.

The Single Market

The single market exercise will be a challenge for the European Community, and a challenge for the United States. We will have to respond quickly and ably. And we don't underestimate the many difficult issues we will be facing—we faced a number of difficult issues and problems when Spain and Portugal acceded to the Community. We will face many more as the single market exercise unfolds.

Our best insurance will be the successful completion of the Uruguay Round of the GATT. It is particularly important that we extend the GATT to cover areas such as services, investment, and intellectual property. A new workable GATT agreement on services would eliminate any perceived need for reciprocity, and to the extent that the European Community wants to use 1992 to open foreign markets, they should work through and be consistent with the GATT. GATT also affords us an opportunity to clarify and improve rules of origin and standards.

"An open single market could help pave the way for 45 more years of world economic integration."

Finally, I would like to place 1992 in a larger context: that of the future international economic environment.

We are at a rather unusual moment in history. The principles that have guided Western economic policies over the past 45 years have been vigorously affirmed. China and the Soviet Union have admitted that the centrally planned, autarkic model has failed. Less developed countries that were denouncing foreign investment as imperialism 10 years ago are now actively courting foreign investors. The extraordinary success of countries such as Korea, Taiwan, and Singapore have demonstrated that outward orientation—joining the global economy—is the key to success.

But even as we have won the war, we continue to struggle. Industrialized nations are flirting with protectionism, and some in the United States view foreign investment as a possible threat. Even many of those countries which have benefited most from a liberal trading system are reluctant to open their own markets rapidly.

It is important that we view 1992 in this context. An open single market could help pave the way for 45 more years of world economic integration. And the most compelling argument for this is the enormous success we have achieved over the past 45 years.

On the other hand, if 1992 is implemented in a closed or protectionist manner, it would cast a pall over the future, giving succor to those that would prefer isolation, self-sufficiency, and protectionism. If 1992 results in an inward-looking European Community, it could prompt others to respond in kind. The United States, as the world's largest exporter, has strong reason to want to avoid this disturbing outcome.

Critical Issues

Nineteen-ninety-two will be a difficult undertaking for the EC-12. They have made a good start, but there are a lot of difficult and critical issues remaining—issues that are important to the United States. The EC Council has approved over 100 of the nearly 300 directives, but some of the questions that will define the new Commission in 1992, and well beyond, have not yet been addressed. These include the harmonization of value added taxes, a single currency and a common central bank, and the free movement of labor, by inference a common immigration policy. It will be fascinating to watch as the debate on these issues unfolds.

Nineteen-ninety-two is an important world event, one in which the United States should be vigilant—vigilant but positive. Too often, 1992 is perceived, in the United States and elsewhere, as an exercise in which we have to be defensive—that we should be worried. We must be engaged with the European Community as it pursues 1992, but that engagement should be based primarily on the basis of opportunity—how much the world will profit if 1992 is outward looking and open. The United States is committed to working with the EC nations, and others, to help see that our shared vision becomes reality.

Eugene J. McAllister is the assistant secretary in the Bureau of Economic and Business Affairs in the Department of State.

"What will make the U.S. dispute with post-1992 Europe different . . . is that it will result from a clash of political, not economic, interests."

viewpoint **18**

A Unified Europe Will Hurt U.S. Interests

George Szamuely

In 1988, Margaret Thatcher went to the College of Europe in Bruges to deliver a skeptical address about developments within the European Economic Community (EEC). Having, she declared, rolled back the frontiers of the state in Britain, she did not want "to see them reimposed at a European level, with a European superstate exercising a new dominance from Brussels." She went on to ridicule the "utopian goals" of the European Commission (EC)—the body entrusted with the preparation, proposal, and execution of new laws and policies for the Community. And she concluded with a call for "a Europe which plays its full part in the wider world, which looks outward not inward, and which preserves that Atlantic community—that Europe on both sides of the Atlantic—which is our noblest inheritance and our greatest strength."

Mrs. Thatcher's words received scant attention in the United States, and that is a pity. The 1992 presidential election here will take place just a few weeks before the deadline that the European Commission has set for the fall of the last of the non-tariff trade barriers among member-countries of the Community. Given the current American preoccupation with unfair trading practices, whether they be those of Japan, Brazil, or India, there is bound to be much discussion in that year's election campaign about the way American high technology is being kept out of the European market; but the enormous *political* implications raised by Mrs. Thatcher's speech, which are more important by far, will very likely be ignored.

There is nothing inherently disastrous about removing non-tariff trade barriers. To the contrary—by 1992, thirty-five years will have passed since the signing of the Treaty of Rome which set up the EEC as an open marketplace, and the current proposals are

no more than a somewhat belated implementation of that agreement. Indeed, Mrs. Thatcher herself has expressed no objections to the 1992 project as such.

Nor is the issue simply one of the likely consequences for American business of the various devices now being introduced precisely in order to keep that business out of Europe. Industrialists from around the country have already been complaining on Capitol Hill about the secretiveness with which Europeans are setting about harmonizing their technical and safety standards, about the onerousness of the new testing and certification regulations, about the local-content and rules-of-origin restrictions that will apply in government procurement preferences, and about the imposition of import and anti-dumping duties. No doubt these businessmen are right to complain, and they will probably succeed in squeezing some concessions out of the Europeans in the inevitably acrimonious battles that are going to take place in the current ("Uruguay") round of GATT (General Agreement on Tariffs and Trade) negotiations.

But what will make the U.S. dispute with post-1992 Europe different from the dispute with Japan, say, or South Korea, is that it will result from a clash of political, not economic, interests. Proof of this can be found in the wave of "Euromania"—inseparable, often, from its better-known relative, "Gorbomania"—now sweeping the Western half of the continent. This movement unites the most disparate elements.

The European Left

On the one hand, there are the spokesmen for the corporate boardrooms as well as the European bureaucrats ensconced in Brussels, who proclaim in ever more apocalyptic terms that the proposed single market is the continent's last chance in an economic war of survival with the United States and Japan. It is not enough, they say, for the internal trade barriers to disappear; urgent measures must be adopted to

George Szamuely, "The Politics of Europe 1992." Reprinted from *Commentary,* October 1989, by permission; all rights reserved.

ensure collaboration among European multinationals to undertake a full-scale restructuring and rationalization of industry in order to create gigantic Euro-firms churning out mass Euro-goods, and, in short, to do whatever is necessary to enable Europe's high-technology industries to take on their rivals. Corporatism on the national level is thus to be replaced by corporatism on the supranational level.

On the other and ultimately more significant hand, there is the European Left, which in recent years has evinced a no less remarkable enthusiasm for the European Community. The program of the Italian Communist party, for instance, urges strongly that the Community cease to be a mere economic organization and become a "political entity" with "real elements of supranationalism." The British Labor party, which actually fought the 1983 general election promising immediate withdrawal from the Community, now waxes lyrical about its virtues.

"To many among Europe's post-Vietnam generation, America is an aging, nagging relative, living off old memories and out of touch with the modern world."

It is not hard to see why. As a result of the Single European Act, which the twelve member-nations signed in 1985 and which came into force in 1987, the powers of the common European institutions are greatly enhanced vis-à-vis individual sovereign governments. The Act has aggrandized the power of the European Commission, while that of the Council of Ministers, for years the symbol of de Gaulle's *l'Europe des patries*, in which individual governments could veto a proposed piece of legislation, has correspondingly declined.

Under Jacques Delors, the former French Socialist Finance Minister, the Commission has taken it upon itself to push through the kind of agenda that most Europeans have been rejecting in recent national elections. In the offing, for example, are measures designed to strengthen labor unions at the expense of management. So-called "common social policies" are also now being worked out whereby the poorer, lower-wage countries of the Community will be compelled to undertake much more costly social programs (in order to protect the highly trade-unionized industries located mainly in the wealthier northern half from "unfair" competition).

On top of all this, the Single European Act has increased the powers of the European Assembly in Strasbourg. Even before the elections to that body in June 1989, the combined forces of European political conservatism held the slenderest of majorities over the Left in the Strasbourg Assembly; now that edge has disappeared, with the socialists and the Greens,

together with the Communists, emerging as a voting bloc capable of pushing through an amalgam of an old Left/New Left agenda.

Three Goals

The single European Act of 1985 committed its signatories to pursue three goals. The first was the "European union." The second was the "social dimension." And the third was "European external identity."

"European union" has clearly meant different things at different times ever since the creation of the European Coal and Steel Community in 1950. In its present usage it refers to the project of establishing, by 1992, a single gigantic internal market of 320 million consumers. The impulse behind it, however, has much less to do with a commitment to free enterprise—otherwise, Mrs. Thatcher would hardly be protesting so much— as with a determination to turn the Community into a trading bloc rivaling the Americans and the Japanese.

The "social dimension," as spelled out by Jacques Delors, is simple *dirigisme*, and it will presumably culminate in his stated goal of ensuring that within ten years, 80 percent of the economic, tax, and social legislation of individual member countries will be decided in Brussels.

As for "European external identity," it is daily becoming clearer how, and against whom, Western Europeans intend to define themselves. Gone from public life in Europe are those symbols which once gave expression to the shared experiences, memories, and sense of purpose that held the West together. The Berlin airlift, the Marshall Plan, the creation of NATO [North Atlantic Treaty Organization], the defeat of the Communist challenge in France and Italy have been replaced in the European mind by the battle over the Euromissiles, the squabbling over the Soviet gas-pipeline deal, or sanctions against Poland. Today, to many among Europe's post-Vietnam generation, America is an aging, nagging relative, living off old memories and out of touch with the modern world. That modern world is, of course, represented by Mikhail Sergeyevich Gorbachev.

A Common European Home

Here we come to perhaps the most important contributing factor to the shaping of a "European external identity." Indeed, the Soviet leader's book, *Perestroika*, might almost have been intended as bedtime reading for Jacques Delors's new European man. In that book Gorbachev complains, for instance, about the "onslaught of 'mass culture' from across the Atlantic"; he worries that the "profoundly intelligent and inherently humane European culture is retreating to the background before the primitive revelry of violence and pornography and the flood of cheap feelings and low thoughts"; he hopes for the "better use of the aggregate potential of Europe for the benefit of its peoples, and in relations with the rest of the world"; and he invokes constantly his well-known theme of a "common European home."

When it comes to specific suggestions, Gorbachev seems, again, to be addressing himself to precisely those economic fears which brought the 1992 project into being. He calls for "research in the fields of superconductivity and biotechnology," for "utilizing thermonuclear energy," for the "joint exploration . . . of outer space." He cites with approval "Giulio Andreotti's idea of a 'world laboratory' " (whatever that may mean). And he offers Soviet help in the West European campaign to keep up with American high technology. Human and natural resources, and gigantic industrial plants, are to be made available to Europe's scientists; all the Europeans have to provide is the research. Farther down the line, there is the tantalizing prospect of the Soviet and East European markets.

"The upshot is that in 1993 or shortly thereafter the United States will likely be confronted with a corporatist, socialist Europe . . . and a Europe with which the U.S. will not be on especially good terms."

A Europe from the Urals to the Atlantic would comprise a market not of 320 million consumers, but of 820 million. It would account for something like 49 percent of the world's GNP [Gross National Product] (as against the United States's 29 percent). Is it reasonable to expect, in this era of new thinking, common policies, shared programs, and restructuring, that the European Community would reject such an offer out of hand, particularly when it comes with an added incentive? That incentive, of course, is the prospect of drastically reduced defense expenditures.

The upshot is that in 1993 or shortly thereafter the United States will likely be confronted with a corporatist socialist Europe—a Europe intricately involved in joint ventures, loans, and special projects with the Soviet bloc, and a Europe with which the U.S. will not be on especially good terms. Nor will Americans be in a position to complain. For it was the U.S. that did more than even the Europeans themselves to create the European Community.

Alliance and Unity

Two aims were being pursued here—the preservation of the Western alliance, and the achievement of European unity. At first these appeared to be mutually reinforcing goals. To preserve the alliance, there was the integrated military command of NATO, with its headquarters first in

Paris and then in Brussels, with its Supreme Commander who was always an American and its Secretary-General who was always a European. And to work for European unity—the only possible aim, so the argument went, for a continent torn apart by a half-century of wars among rival nation states—there was that series of first steps, the Coal and Steel Community (1950), the European Economic Community (1957), and the European Atomic Energy Commission (1957). These were to lead to a new political federation—the United States of Europe—which would in turn provide the necessary underpinning for the military hardware of NATO. . . .

It was only with the advent of the Nixon administration that a change in American attitudes could be discerned. What provoked it was not just de Gaulle's continuing attacks on U.S. foreign policy from Vietnam to Latin America, or his withdrawal from NATO's integrated military command. There was something more ominous at work. Then, as now, Europeans were convinced that they were being "colonized" by the United States, and in particular by the American multinationals. Consequently, when de Gaulle began to exchange France's dollar reserves for gold, thereby hoping to force a devaluation of the dollar and make American investment in Europe that much more difficult, he was cheered from all sides. The European Left approved a move that seemed directed against the "multinationals"; the Right applauded a blow at the "Americanization of Europe"; the corporatists were happy that foreign enterprises were being prevented from interfering with national economic plans.

An Economic Cold War

In 1969 Maurice Stans, Nixon's Secretary of Commerce, delared an intention to "mount a full-scale counterattack" on EEC non-tariff trade barriers. The following year, decrying Europe's attitude to the "economic problems and the political and military burdens carried by the U.S.," the American ambassador to the EEC spoke in terms of "irritation, frustration, and a brooding sense of apprehension." The White House economic-policy adviser, Francis Bator, said there was no "way to avoid an economic cold war between a growing EEC and ourselves." For the first time it seemed that the European Community, far from being a pillar of the Atlantic alliance, might be on its way to becoming a battering ram for breaking it up.

Nixon's Secretary of State, Henry Kissinger, was one of the first to perceive the coming dangers. As he later wrote in his memoirs:

> We were essentially agnostic about how and when political cohesion came about, provided it did not seek its identity in opposing us. And yet that is precisely the concept of European unity that was gaining ground. Those European leaders most dedicated to European unity were beginning to perceive a conflict between Atlantic unity and

European identity. European unification was absorbing more of their energies and dedication than was the elaboration of Atlantic institutions.

Today, twenty years later, Kissinger's apprehensions are being borne out in plain view. Worse yet, the internal political dynamics in almost every EC-member country are leading it away from Atlanticism.

Green Politics

West Germany—the motor of the Community, accounting for 26 percent of its GNP—is undergoing political turmoil. Current polls put the Social Democrats (SPD) and the Greens ahead of the Christian Democrats (CDU), the Christian Social Union (CSU), and the Free Democrats (FDP). Moreover, even if the Germans balk at the prospect of being governed by a "Red-Green" coalition, the Social Democrats could well return to power following the 1990 elections if, as seems increasingly likely, Hans-Dietrich Genscher's Free Democrats desert Chancellor Kohl's coalition. An SPD-FDP government led probably by Oskar Lafontaine—a politician who came to national prominence in the early 1980's as an ardent foe of NATO and nuclear power—would be a far cry from the days when the SPD used to be led by Helmut Schmidt. Today's SPD is fanatically anti-nuclear and also maintains close interparty links with the Communist parties of Eastern Europe. In any case, disillusionment with Atlanticism is rampant through all sectors of the population. German crowds mobbed Gorbachev during his visit while President Bush was berated by government officials over the issue of low-flying NATO aircraft. The brief twenty-year interlude of *Westpolitik* is now definitely at an end, its place taken by *Drang nach Osten*.

"The internal political dynamics in almost every EC-member country are leading it away from Atlanticism."

Meanwhile the French are pushing the post-1992 Community in a corporatist-socialist direction. In general, the 1992 project is largely a French brainchild, having come about as a result of François Mitterrand's doomed 1981-83 experiment with "socialism in one country." But the lesson the French President drew from those two disastrous years was not that the market should determine the allocation of capital and goods, but that for socialism to succeed it has to be implemented on a Europe-wide scale. Jacques Delors, the Finance Minister during those turbulent times, expresses the egalitarian side of it with his "social dimension" and "fundamental charter of social rights," while Laurent Fabius, who as Prime Minister from 1984 to 1986 inaugurated the French public rhetoric of computers, videodiscs, and the

"Silicon Valley spirit" and who headed the French list in June 1989's elections to the European parliament, represents the corporatist side.

What remains unclear is what will happen in Britain. Since 1988, Margaret Thatcher vigorously led the fight against the Delors regime in Brussels. Yet her own party is divided on the issue; indeed, much of the British political establishment is, and has always been, passionately Europhile and has thus taken a dim view of her recent activities. Moreover, she received a rebuff at the hands of the electorate in the June 1989 elections when Labor came back strong.

Even if Mrs. Thatcher has been uncompromising on introducing socialism by the back door in Europe, she has sounded an uncertain note on Gorbachev. At times, the Prime Minister has praised the Soviet leader fulsomely, going so far as to declare the cold war at an end. At other times, she has warned her countrymen and other Europeans not to be taken in by the siren song from the East. Such inconsistency can lead to trouble, as became evident during the run-up to the NATO summit, when her strong line on the modernization of tactical nuclear missiles elicited little support either among her European counterparts or at home.

Still, Mrs. Thatcher's stand is for the moment the only obstacle to the corporatist-protectionist regime in Brussels, as well as to the neo-socialist agenda enshrined in the European Social Charter. Whether she will be helped by the United States is a crucial question which unfortunately remains open—though President Bush's recent expressions of enthusiasm for European unity, as well as his downgrading of the special relationship with Britain that characterized the Reagan years, are not very reassuring.

George Szamuely is a free-lance writer who contributes to The Wall Street Journal, Insight, *and* Commentary.

"Many Japanese will say that they have already done a great deal to open their market and to be good citizens of the international community."

viewpoint 19

Japanese Culture Makes Trade Disputes Solvable

Takashi Oka

On Aug. 15, 1945, I was a private in the Imperial Japanese Army. To Japanese of my generation, that was surely the most unforgettable day in our lives, the day the Japanese nation was reborn.

I can't help recalling it now as the perception gap across the Pacific Ocean seems to widen while the $50 billion trade gap between Japan and the United States fails to narrow.

"Revisionism" has become the West's polite term for "Japan bashing." But it still challenges the old, comfortable assumption that, as the Japanese economy matures, it will evolve into an American-type, consumer-driven society.

The alternative is a much scarier notion that reawakens images of Pearl Harbor and World War II. The motive-power of Tokyo's relentless export drive, the "revisionist" thinking holds, is economic conquest.

Captured by Diamonds

Yet there are conquests and conquests. To take one small sign of the times, Japan has been captured by diamonds. In 1988 it spent more on them per capita than the US. A couple of decades ago only 6% of Japanese fiancées sported diamond engagement rings; today 77% do. All the brand names of Europe and America fight to get their luxury products onto Japanese department store shelves, because status-conscious Japanese will pay more for the "in" brand than any other people.

Startling larger signs of Japan's opening door were cited by Kazuo Nukazawa, managing director of Japan's most powerful and comprehensive business organization, the Federation of Economic Organizations, in a recent interview:

• From 1985 to 1988 US exports to Japan increased by a higher percentage (67%) than exports to Western Europe (55%).

• Today Japan imports *more* from the US than West Germany, France, and Italy combined. Together these three countries have a population and a GNP (gross national product) greater than the population and GNP of Japan. If Japan's markets are so closed, Nukazawa argued, his country should be importing *less* from the US than these European allies.

• Japan's imports of *manufactured goods* have risen during this period from 30% of total imports to 50%. That's not bad, Nukazawa said, compared to West Germany, where manufactured goods make up 60% of all imports. (Nearly 80% of US imports are manufactured goods.)

Just what has happened to Japan since those World War II Army days when we soldiers lived on a mixture of watery soup and rice mixed with sorghum, eating from bamboo bowls because the usual aluminum utensils had all been smelted down as part of a desperate effort to keep Japan's war factories operating?

As today's debate about Japan goes on—with major effects on the future of world harmony and wealth—the reference point has to be Aug. 15, 1945. . . .

Freedom from Being Special

My first and most overwhelming feeling was immense relief that the long war was over, that Japan would be a nation at peace. The second feeling was more complex. It was that at last for the first time, I was freed from the burden of belonging to a special race, distinct from and superior to all other races. Not every Japanese believed the official doctrine, but it was what we had been brought up on, and the breaking of this myth freed the Japanese to become ordinary members of the human race.

Yet now the revisionists—even when they claim not to be Japan bashers—offer an image of Japan as remaining intractably "different." They say Japan is *not* becoming a more open economy. The standard rules of a free market do *not* work with such an outlaw. In Japan's case the rules have to be *different*.

There doesn't seem to be any agreement as to what these different rules should be. But the general principle seems to be that the American market should be open to Japanese products only to the extent that the Japanese market is open to American products. Super 301, shorthand for the main provision of the omnibus trade law enacted by Congress in the spring of 1989, is seen as the weapon by which to enforce this principle.

Tokyo More Feared than Moscow

Trade disputes between Washington and Tokyo (or, for that matter, London et al. and Tokyo) are nothing new. First textiles, then steel, then cars, and most recently computer chips, to say nothing of beef, oranges, cellular phones, and space satellites.

The cumulative effect over a 20-year period has been to broaden and deepen the controversy until today it extends beyond trade into fundamental aspects of Japanese and US society. . . .

The guru of the revisionist school is Chalmers Johnson, a professor at the University of California's San Diego campus, who coined the phrase "capitalist development state" to describe the kind of country Japan is, and who refers to MITI, Japan's powerful Ministry of International Trade and Industry, as "the Pentagon of Japan." Johnson wrote *MITI and the Japanese Miracle*, a Bible for businessmen seeking a guide through the labyrinth of Japanese officialdom. . . .

"Trade disputes between Washington and Tokyo . . . are nothing new."

Revisionism is said to be gaining ground in the middle reaches of the US government and among congressional staff officers. It is not as yet a single coherent body of doctrine, nor do all revisionists agree on all points with each other. But it starts with an objective fact that is the albatross of US-Japanese relations:

• In 1985 the US trade deficit with Japan was in the range of $50 billion.

• In 1989, it is still in this range, even though in the meantime the US dollar's exchange rate relative to the yen has been halved.

During this period, US exports regained the global competitiveness they had lost during the preceding period of the high dollar; in 1989, for instance, the US again enjoys a surplus in its trade with the European Community.

Why is it that the deficit persists, at such a high level, only with Japan? Is Japan a special case? Do normal market rules not apply to Japan? And the logical extension of these questions is: What kind of

society is Japan?

If Japan is indeed a rogue elephant in the international economic community, then special rules have to be devised to deal with it. The principal industrialized democracies—the US and the European Community—will have to "manage" trade with Japan, meaning that they will broaden and intensify the restraints they are already imposing on certain categories of Japanese exports, such as textiles, steel, and cars.

The revisionists' basic complaint against Japan is that the Japanese market is closed to outsiders, while Japan takes full advantage of the postwar system of free trade to rain exports on the rest of the world, particularly the US. Years of effort have failed to pry open the Japanese market to any significant degree, the revisionists say.

Recently Japan and the US have embarked on a series of talks that goes by the unwieldy title, "Structural Impediments Initiative," or SII. . . .

For Japan's Own Good

Officially, both sides are upbeat about the talks, the stated purpose of which is to uncover and correct structural impediments in the two countries to restoring an acceptable trade balance. The term "structural impediments" gets around Japanese sensitivities by implying that the obstacles are not all on the Japanese side; that the US also has a lot of correcting to do, such as encouraging savings or reducing the $150 billion federal budget deficit.

Nevertheless, the psychological pressure is much more on Japan than it is on the United States. After all, it is the US that is on the deficit side of the trade gap, while Japan is on the surplus side of that gap.

The US has an additional point, which it pressed with great vigor at the first round of the SII talks in Tokyo. The changes it is asking Tokyo to bring about, it says, will certainly help the US; but they will also help the Japanese consumer.

American and other goods have difficulty penetrating the Japanese market partly because the domestic distribution system is unwieldy, with many more intermediaries between the producer and the final customer than in the US. The price structure is weighted in favor of exports and against imports. Japanese cameras, golf clubs— you name it—cost less in the US than they do in Japan, as Japanese tourists going abroad are discovering.

An Economic Monster

Japan is rich today, in terms of dollars, but individual Japanese do not feel rich, because the benefits of the high yen have not been passed on to the consumer. And the quality of life in Japan is poorer than it is in most Western nations. Housing is moderate, while land prices are shockingly high; the social infrastructure—roads, sewers, parks—lags far behind Western Europe or the US.

If Japan would spend more on improving life at home than on so singlemindedly promoting exports abroad, it would pull in more imports from the US and elsewhere and its trade balance would not be so out of whack, US officials say. Americans are puzzled why Japanese voters do not rise up and demand these things. The apparent docility of the Japanese public only confirms the notion that Japan is different, that it is a kind of economic monster.

"Japan is rich today, in terms of dollars, but individual Japanese do not feel rich, because the benefits of the high yen have not been passed on to the consumer."

From the reference point of 1945, however, a broader perspective emerges. Japan is the first non-Western nation to have joined the ranks of the advanced industrialized democracies on the basis of having adopted and to some extent adapted Western institutions. It has been in many ways a lonely, disorienting process, and it still continues today.

The present institutions and value systems of the West grew organically out of Judeo-Christian and Greco-Roman thought. To a Westerner, it may be perfectly natural that these institutions are today considered universal in scope. International law is international law, even if it includes no Confucian or Islamic elements.

But a non-Westerner has to consciously adopt ways of thought that come from outside his own original frame of reference. When the process has continued for over a century, as it has in Japan, it becomes difficult for a Japanese to separate out what is distinctly and exclusively indigenous in his makeup from the expectations he has received from the West.

Increased Imports

A Westerner seeing a Japanese is much more likely to be conscious of the difference, because he can more readily catch what is unfamiliar or inexplicable to him, on the basis of Western logic, in what that Japanese person seems to be thinking and doing.

The pace of change in the 44 years since World War II has been bewildering, the transition in outlook from generation to generation pronounced. Defeat in the war . . . the American occupation . . . the progressive shift from hunger and want to increasing comfort and prosperity . . . the export drives that spewed out Japanese cameras, cars, and computer chips around the globe . . . the material affluence that sucks in fashions from Paris, lobsters from Maine, pet lizards from Papua New Guinea—the mélange of influences coming from within and without has been so indiscriminate that any Japanese would be hard pressed to sort out the Western and non-Western

elements in his or her makeup. He may say proudly that he is 100% Japanese, but except in the ethnic sense it would be impossible for him to say he is 100% non-Western.

Economic Growth

As the engine of economic growth got going the Japanese found their lives getting more comfortable and eventually, for some, downright luxurious. In 1988, Narita airport outstripped New York in the amount of air cargo handled. This is largely because bulky food imports—frozen and fresh tuna, lobsters, prawns, herring roe, mushrooms, tropical fruit—have grown astronomically in volume.

"The higher the price, the better it sells," says a salesman in the Tiffany boutique at Mitsukoshi, Tokyo's oldest department store. But the work habits that produced the cameras, cars, and computers underwriting all this prosperity remain much the same.

"I don't think young people work any less hard than people of my generation," says Tadashi Ono, a 40-year-old junior executive in one of Mazda Corporation's outlets. "But they work for more limited goals. I scrimped and saved to buy my own apartment. The 20-year-olds who work under me save to buy a sports car, or an expensive ski outfit, or an African safari."

And, certainly, within both Ono and his subordinates, there are mental strands that go back to pre-modern times—a deference to authority, a tendency to submerge the individual in the group, a keen sense of competition tempered by the need to conform.

What America Needs to Do

Is the fault for today's economic imbalance all on Japan's side? Tokyo and Washington agree it is not. At the SII talks, the Japanese delegation noted that, if Japan had to do more to help its consumers, the US needed to do more to help its producers:

• American manufacturers are insufficiently export-oriented; they think in terms of immediate profits rather than strategy for the long haul.

• The US savings rate is very low—6.3% compared to 15% in Japan or 13% in West Germany. This is inadequate to cover needed investment; so the funds for such investment have to be borrowed from abroad.

• The federal budget deficit continues at a high level, despite repeated admonitions not only from Japan but also from practically all the US's Western partners.

To turn these statements into practical steps to remove structural impediments is, however, wrenchingly difficult, perhaps more so for Japan than for the US, because it is always easier to close doors than to open them. The first steps—bringing down tariffs, eliminating some of the more egregious regulations that make market penetration difficult for outsiders, tackling the distribution system at least to the extent of making it less cumbersome for supermarket chains to expand their operations—have been or are being implemented. What remains are core issues that are perceived in Tokyo as demanding changes in what makes the Japanese Japanese.

What Japan Has Already Done

Before taking up these core issues, however, many Japanese will say that they have already done a great deal to open their market and to be good citizens of the international community. As part of the agreement reached at the Plaza Hotel in New York in 1985 to let the dollar float downward and the yen upward, Tokyo said it would stimulate domestic demand so as to pull in more imports. It did so through a series of supplementary budgets promoting public works, the effect of which was to sharply reduce the share of exports in the annual growth of gross national product. In 1988, domestic demand contributed 6% to GNP growth, while exports contributed a negative 1%. As a result, GNP grew by 5%, all of which was due to growth in domestic demand.

As for that $50 billion trade gap, the Japanese of course admit that it persists, but they ask for recognition that Japan's imports from the US have increased substantially. The trade gap persists because Japan's exports, both overall and to the US, have increased by more than Japan's imports. Some economists worry that a rich-invest-more effect may make the trade gap last well into the future. Japanese industries are investing far more in research and retooling than their US counterparts. So, even though the Japanese are increasingly buying American, US consumers show no signs of resisting the improved products resulting from all that Japanese investing.

To return to director Nukazawa of the Federation of Economic Organizations, he asserted that the US is not as great an upholder of free trade as Americans sometimes think. About half of Japan's exports to the US are subject to some form of restriction, he said—in other words, of managed trade.

"I really do not like the moral indignation which the Americans express to us," he exploded. "They are not in such a lofty position. They are not in a position to throw stones at us."

Most Japanese economists readily admit that Japan has prospered by following the rules of the US market when it exported goods to that market. Basically the US market is open.

Japan's Rules

But Americans exporting to Japan find a market hedged about with so many rules and regulations, so many unwritten practices, that many give up in disgust and loudly complain that, for all the market-opening measures Japan has taken over the years, the Japanese market is closed.

And when their Japanese counterparts argue that

these regulations do not discriminate against Americans, that any new Japanese enterprise has to surmount the same hurdles, American irritation is only exacerbated. Such arguments are seen as an excuse for continuing and even expanding Japan's already huge trade surplus with the US.

There are two possible answers: Close the US's market to the same degree as Japan's; or open the Japanese market to the same degree as the American. The Bush administration has opted for the second course, and is consistently and repeatedly asking Japan to open its market further. In so doing, of course, the US runs a risk. A number of years ago, William Brock, then the chief US trade representative, said he had a recurring nightmare: The Japanese would do everything the Americans asked of them, and still the US-Japan trade gap would remain. . . .

"Bulky food imports—frozen and fresh tuna, lobsters, prawns, herring roe, mushrooms, tropical fruit—have grown astronomically in volume."

Some Japanese officials say privately that the US is being cynical. It knows that Japan cannot ever be open to exactly the same degree as America, and is therefore merely looking for an excuse to impose protectionist measures against the Japanese. To such officials, there is a line beyond which Japan cannot and should not go.

"Our system works. Why should we change it to please you?" is their attitude. If persisted in, it will lead to a severe clash of cultures. Some say this has already begun.

But there is a deeper dimension to this dispute—one that gives cause for hope that a new basis can be found for a more solid partnership across the Pacific. That dimension starts with the recognition that Japan and the US are indeed different but that neither is static—both countries are moving. The next step is to try to ensure that the movement is in a direction that lessens differences and makes remaining contrasts tolerable. In the final stage, both sides should be able to cry, "Vive la différence!"—for nonadversarial differences only indicate the infinite variety and renewability of the human race.

Takashi Oka was an international correspondent for The Christian Science Monitor. *He now covers East Asia from Tokyo for the* World Monitor.

"U.S. officials will never understand the true inner workings of Japan's group culture, so they shouldn't negotiate on details."

Japanese Culture Makes Trade Disputes Unsolvable

James Flanigan

The Bush Administration cited Japan for unfair trade practices on supercomputers, satellites and lumber in May 1989. But the real focus was not on particular products—it was on a whole economic system.

Ultimately, the U.S. action stemmed from the growing belief that Japan's economy is geared to what is called adversarial trade—importing reluctantly but exporting aggressively. That's a way of benefiting from the other fellow's market but denying him the benefit of your own—a particularly galling fault when the offender is a big economic power like Japan.

The Bush Administration, which is proposing talks with Japan on impediments to trade, is asking its Asian ally to shoulder the responsibilities that go with being a major nation, to grow up and no longer try to live at the expense of others.

Japan's trade surpluses are unique. It sells more than it buys just about everywhere. To West Germany—one of the world's great exporters—Japan sells $14 billion worth of goods but buys only $6 billion worth. To the European Community, Japan sells roughly $20 billion more than it buys; it sells more to Asia than it buys, and more to Latin America, and much more to the United States—which accounts for 37% of Japan's exports.

Adversarial Trade

Both friends and critics of Japan have acknowledged that it practices adversarial trade—a term coined by Peter F. Drucker, a longtime friend and adviser to Japanese industry. Drucker warned Japan at the time that keeping its markets closed while taking advantage of others would bring a reaction.

Now to some extent it has, although Sen. Lloyd Bentsen (D.Tex.) criticized the Administration's action

as "only a first step" that Japan already had been "able to water down."

But reaction has been growing. Where for years Japan was admired for its hard work and industry, today its very system is being seen as a problem. In *Politics and Productivity,* a new book edited by University of California scholars Chalmers Johnson, Laura D'Andrea Tyson and John Zysman, the industrial policy that raised a defeated and hungry Japan to the heights of prosperity in a few decades is seen as a disturbing model for developing nations and a problem for the United States.

Other recent commentators have less kind things to say. One new book, *The Enigma of Japanese Power* by Karel van Wolferen, a Dutch journalist who has lived for 25 years in Japan, sees its industrial complex as a danger to itself and to the rest of the world. And the same thought is taken up by American journalist James Fallows in an *Atlantic* magazine article titled "Containing Japan," using a term for America's chief Asian ally that formerly was reserved for its principal ideological and military adversary, the Soviet Union.

Trade Barriers

The focus of all that criticism is much more than traditional trade matters— tariffs and other barriers. The charge is that Japan's true trade barriers lie in its closed system of corporations, particularly the way its big companies organize in groups, hold each other's stock and coordinate business activities. Here, that would be against U.S. antitrust laws; there, it's standard business practice.

Groups are no secret. About 100 of Japan's largest and best-known corporations belong to six groups of companies connected to banks or finance houses. The Mitsui group, for example, consists of 24 companies, including such familiar names as Toshiba and Toyota. The 21-company Sumitomo group includes NEC, the world's largest semiconductor maker.

The Dai-Ichi Kangyo Group includes Hitachi, a

giant electrical and computer company, as well as Fujitsu, Japan's leading computer maker, and 45 other big companies that in total employ 500,000 people and have total sales of 44 trillion yen—or $338 billion, slightly more than the combined revenues of General Motors, IBM and Exxon.

> "U.S. companies or trade officials may press all they want for sales in Japan, but a group member's supercomputer or semiconductor comes first."

What do groups do? "Representatives of the group meet every three months to exchange information on business opportunities and, where applicable, to coordinate their companies' activities," says Dai-Ichi Kangyo in its annual report. They give preference to other group members in purchasing and trade business information.

To a Japanese observer such interconnections are no big deal. The six big groups, with 182 companies, are only the top level of a structure of business among Japan's estimated 1.7 million companies, in which small firms serve big ones, and big companies have a responsibility for the well-being of the small—"as feudal lords and vassals had mutual obligations," explains Bob Ching, the Shanghai-born head of Asian operations for Boston Consulting, who served 11 years in Japan.

The groups are "the tip of the iceberg of the shared purpose and vision that one feels in Japanese industry," says William Ouchi, professor of management at the UCLA graduate business school. "What lies under the surface is a series of networks—financial networks and government-business networks, scientific networks and political and educational networks that jointly provide the interstitial tissue that knits it all together."

Companies within the groups hold stock in each other—between 15% and 30% on average of a group member's shares are held by other members, providing a stable source of ownership for group companies.

Cross-share holding, familiar from an earlier era in American business—when for example Du Pont held General Motors shares for decades—is common in Japan and thought to be a good idea by many U.S. business people.

Capital Investments

Toyota owns more than 20% of the stock of Nippondenso and Aisin Seiko, its major parts suppliers, as a form of pledge or bond. The investment assures the supplier that if he makes capital investments—which ultimately benefit Toyota cars—he won't be left in the lurch by the big company. U.S. car companies now are offering suppliers similar pledges by means of long-term contracts.

"The Japanese have a good understanding of supplier relationships," says James Morgan, founder and president of Applied Materials, a Santa Clara, Calif., company that makes semiconductor manufacturing equipment. Fujitsu, for example, owns 21% of Advantest, a principal semiconductor equipment supplier. But Advantest supplies Fujitsu's competitors, too. Why does Fujitsu permit that? "So they remain strong," explains a Fujitsu executive. "If they are weak, they are no good to us."

That's nice, say trade experts, but a country that seeks to benefit from free markets internationally can't fall back on group behavior at home. Both the U.S. and Japanese economies are theoretically open, says UC Berkeley business professor Michael Gerlach, but the word means different things when firms of one country habitually buy from one another and ignore bids from foreign competitors.

Bluntly put, U.S. companies or trade officials may press all they want for sales in Japan, but a group member's supercomputer or semiconductor comes first.

Trade Discrimination

U.S. semiconductors, for example, go in the motors of all the world's cars—except Japanese cars. "Where we take 70% U.S. semiconductors," says the head of one U.S. car company, "the Japanese maker will take less than 1%." Why take any? Because the U.S. industry is technologically ahead in many semiconductor products. "The Japanese will only buy what they absolutely cannot make themselves," says Robert Noyce, a U.S. semiconductor industry pioneer.

Sometimes discrimination against the U.S. supplier seems comic, as in the episode of Motorola's cellular phones. The Japanese government, in an ostensible example of encouraging free trade and competition, gave out cellular telephone specifications for a partnership including Motorola, and one including Toyota. Toyota got the Tokyo-Osaka corridor through the populous heart of Japan; Motorola got the hinterland.

So the question on trade has become not whether Japan imports another supercomputer, but whether it changes its closed system. And to penetrate the system, trade advisers who have gained influence recently, such as former Commerce Department official Clyde Prestowitz, counsel the broad approach. Clearly, say these analysts, U.S. officials will never understand the true inner workings of Japan's group culture, so they shouldn't negotiate on details. Instead, they advise, require Japan to give U.S. products the same market share Japan's products enjoy here. And let Japan work out ways to meet broad targets, they argue; it is the trading partner that must change.

Which raises the question, Why should Japan change when its system has brought it success? The answer, say many experts, including Japanese officials, is that the price of Japan's success is coming out of the hides of its own people.

Prices in Japan are high in order to provide a home market cushion of profit for Japanese companies competing in international trade. Buyers in Tokyo pay more so foreign customers in New York can pay less for Canon cameras, or Hitachi (Sears, RCA) TV sets and VCRs. Japanese telephone users pay more for phone calls than do Americans, so that suppliers to Nippon Telegraph & Telephone can support overseas business with home market profits. In the modernization of the phone system, prices being paid for fiber-optic cable are three times the world price—because Japanese cable suppliers are uncompetitive except in their home market.

That's why economists figure the Japanese people, despite the strong yen and the fact that they have the world's highest gross national product per person at $17,244, have 30% less purchasing power than the currency's strength should warrant. That is, the Japanese people have lower purchasing power than they should because the goods are not available or they are unaffordable—as housing is in big cities.

The blame for that situation lies more in politics than economics, says Naohiro Amaya, a former vice minister of Japan's renowned Ministry of International Trade and Industry (MITI) and one of the chief planners of his country's postwar development. "After the war we put more emphasis on economic values than political values of freedom and democracy—but modern economies need democratic society," says Amaya. "Of course we pay respect to the ideals of freedom and democracy, but in everyday life they are not implemented. If freedom prevailed, prices would go down."

Economic Freedom

Amaya equates political freedom with economic freedom—the principle that allowing products to compete freely and consumers to choose is the most just and democratic way to allocate resources in society.

Amaya is also saying Japan has unfinished business. "We are facing the question of what sort of relations we are going to have with the outside world and, domestically, what sort of political ideals we are going to pursue." Now retired from government and serving as executive director of the Dentsu Institute for Human Studies, Amaya argues that if Japan is to change, its people will have to demand it.

Yet the country's whole image and demeanor seem to refute him. In a time of restructuring in the West and *perestroika* in the East, Japan seems like a song from the 1950s. Big companies rule its business undisturbed, as elderly politicians survive the Recruit scandal and carry on quietly arranging things behind the scenes. Protest is scarcely seen or heard, even though millions of middle-class salary earners now reckon they will never be able to afford to buy a home.

Why are the Japanese people so apparently uncomplaining? Because rising standards of living since the war are better than anything that went before; Japan has always been a tough place to live. "One of the most difficult things for Americans to understand is the Japanese lack of opportunity," says Jiro Tokuyama, senior adviser to the Mitsui Foundation and a Tokyo- and Harvard-educated, longtime student of the two societies. Japan is not only crowded, it is competitive; it has 120 million people living in a country the size of California (28 million population), and in the postwar years, 40 out of every 100 of them graduate from college and want good jobs. Before the war and throughout Japanese history, most of the people lived in villages, yet in the cities before the war, labor relations were violent.

"The question on trade has become not whether Japan imports another supercomputer, but whether it changes its closed system."

Japan's postwar solution was the corporate system, with a hierarchy of organizations and assured employment. It was stable, but also static. A man didn't move from company to company, and companies didn't hire talent away from each other.

Closed Systems

But closed systems are challenged when conditions change. And change is occurring today as foreign firms demand a place in the Japanese market and Japanese companies move to foreign markets. Employees in new fields such as financial services are changing employers these days as premiums are paid to attract specialists and experts. "The group system is changing," says Minoru Makihara, president of New York-based Mitsubishi International Corp.

Companies are trimming staff, setting up dozens, even hundreds, of subsidiaries, often solely for the purpose of getting surplus employees off the payroll. Japan is seeing an entrepreneurial wave as members of the Japanese baby boom— those born during a population surge in the 1950s—are reaching 35 to 39 years old and hearing "up or out" at their companies.

And companies are changing to get more efficient and competitive for world markets—a surprise perhaps to many Americans who tend to overestimate Japan's industry. The fact is, for all the sheltering and group cooperation, results overseas for Japanese companies have been mixed. Automobiles have been a big success, but telecommunications has not.

Similarly, despite advance publicity about their great size, Japanese financial companies have made negligible strides in financial services worldwide. The size of Japan's brokerage houses, in any case, results from the fact that fixed commissions—and the profits they bring through restricted competition—are still in force in Japan as they have not been since 1975 in the United States.

The comforts of the home market have made Japanese industry reluctant to go abroad before now. Although Japan accounts for almost 20% of the world's industrial output, and its exports account for 10% of world trade, its companies on average have less than 5% of their production outside of Japan. This compares to 15% to 20% for West Germany, Britain and other major nations, and 17% for U.S. business. "It's still a developing economy," says Drucker of Japan today.

"Japan has been able to make its economic strides and practice adversarial trade without world retaliation, because it had both a big protector and a big customer in the United States."

So it may be, because the Bush Administration gave Japan notice that it's time to move on, as one would to an aging adolescent. For four decades now, Japan has been able to make its economic strides and practice adversarial trade without world retaliation, because it had both a big protector and a big customer in the United States. Now that protector and customer is demanding a change, asking Japan to look beyond its own needs and face new responsibility. That's what the whole trade thing is about, not trade war but trade maturity.

James Flanigan is a staff writer for the daily newspaper, the Los Angeles Times.

"Moynihan's bombshell will center on two . . . giant constituencies: America's work force and the mammoth baby-boom generation."

viewpoint 21

The Moynihan Plan to Cut Social Security Taxes: An Overview

Susan Dentzer

Just when it seemed the 1990 budget debate would hinge largely on a fight over capital-gains taxes, a free-for-all over Social Security levies has blown the battle wide open. The proposal by Senator Daniel Patrick Moynihan to slash payroll taxes for 132 million workers has reopened old wounds from earlier wars over the sacrosanct Social Security system. But while those struggles were aimed at winning the hearts and minds of America's elderly, the coming clash over Moynihan's bombshell will center on two other giant constituencies: America's work force and the mammoth baby-boom generation. The fight could change the face of U.S. fiscal policy for years to come.

Moynihan's plan would end the buildup of surpluses in Social Security's trust funds to help pay for the retirement of the baby boom—a strategy the New York Democrat had long favored—and call a halt to government's looting of those reserves to help finance other spending. In fiscal 1991 alone, workers would get a tax cut equal to $55 billion and would be spared billions of dollars more in taxes in years hence. Unless offset by other tax hikes or deep budget cuts, this huge tax cut would widen the federal budget deficit: some analysts warned that it could cause economic havoc, fueling inflation and forcing the Federal Reserve into a dangerous round of money tightening. To forestall disaster, George Bush could be forced to agree to deeper defense cuts and much forsworn new taxes, or reach a compromise to carry out long-term deficit cutting to protect the Social Security reserves. Without such a deal, even Bush's cherished capital-gains-tax cut seems endangered. "How can the President claim Moynihan's tax cut is bad because it goes for workers, but his own tax cut is good because it goes for capitalists?" asks Brookings Institution economist Barry Bosworth.

The issues raised by Moynihan could also prompt a serious look at the trend to finance growing shares of government spending through regressive payroll taxes on workers. For the past five decades, the payroll tax has followed what economist Eugene Steuerle calls "a simple rule of thumb," rising 3 percentage points each decade, to its current level of 15.3 percent. Counting employers' share of the payroll tax—which economists assume workers actually bear in the form of reduced wages—3 out of 4 Americans now pay more in taxes to finance Social Security and medicare than they pay in income taxes. Because the tax largely exempts fringe benefits, it may also discriminate against part-time workers, women and minorities, who tend to earn most of their compensation in cash. As Congress probes these inequities, sweeping changes to spread the burden of payroll taxes could lie ahead.

Scare Tactics

Even before lawmakers returned to Washington from their extended holiday recess, it was clear that Moynihan's plan held the power to reshape old political fault lines. Bush called the proposal a "charade," then fell back on old scare tactics, suggesting—falsely—that Moynihan's plan would lead to cutbacks in benefits affecting "the older people in this country." While Democratic congressional leaders were still pondering their position, some key legislators in both parties also joined Bush in denouncing the plan. "The decision to put something aside for the babyboomers was probably the only act of fiscal responsibility during the Reagan years, so repealing it would make the record perfect," snorted Representative Andy Jacobs (D-Ind.), who chairs a House subcommittee on Social Security. Senator John Heinz (R-Pa.) warned that Moynihan's changes would "undermine people's confidence and risk the soundness of the Social Security system."

But other lawmakers heartily endorsed Moynihan's plan. Some Democrats crowed that it would shore up the party's support among younger workers, and many Republicans voiced their approval as well. Indeed, it appeared that "the only constituency against this thing is absolutely inside the Beltway," said former Senate Budget Committee staffer Steve Bell. Lining up in favor were conservative tax-cut enthusiasts, small businesses hard hit by the payroll tax and groups skeptical that the government could keep its hands off the reserves, such as the nascent 1,000-member American Association of Boomers and even the vocal senior citizens' group, the National Committee to Preserve Social Security and Medicare. The potent American Association of Retired Persons was reserving judgment until it heard more details of Moynihan's plan.

Despite its official opposition, moreover, even the White House was divided internally over the substance of the senator's proposal. While Budget Director Richard Darman had so far won the argument against it, sources said there was keen interest in a big tax cut among supply-siders and conservatives like White House Chief of Staff John Sununu. Behind closed doors, "there's a lot of mixed feelings" about the Moynihan plan, acknowledges one White House aide.

"With the program facing insolvency in 1977 and again in 1983, Moynihan and other legislators pushed up payroll-tax rates and nudged the system in the direction of a pension fund."

For staunch Social Security defender Moynihan, who in 1989 termed the system's growing reserves America's key to "a very bright future," the proposal represented a change of heart born of desperation. For years, Social Security had operated more or less on a pay-as-you-go basis, collecting just about enough in payroll taxes each year to pay benefits to current retirees. But with the program facing insolvency in 1977 and again in 1983, Moynihan and other legislators pushed up payroll-tax rates and nudged the system in the direction of a pension fund, in which resources to pay out future benefits are built up well in advance. The move was prompted by a grim demographic reckoning: An estimated 70 million babyboomers faced retirement beginning about 2010, even as the ratio of future workers to retirees was destined to slump sharply. It seemed questionable that tomorrow's shrunken work force could tolerate the steep payroll taxes needed to fund a pay-as-you-go system.

The resulting decision to prefund partially the baby-boomers' benefits was based on elegant economic theory. As payroll taxes rolled in, the growing reserves would be invested in special

Treasury bonds, or government IOU's, effectively cutting the outstanding national debt. In effect, the reserves would amount to a form of national savings, freeing up other private capital for companies to borrow in order to invest in new plants and technology. That new equipment would help raise workers' productivity and along with it their wages. When it came time for government to pay back the IOU's so that boomers could get their benefits, the 21st-century work force would be so well off that it could readily bear large payroll levies or hefty income taxes.

The Government Raid

Ever since the adoption of the prefunding plan, economists have debated its merits with the intensity of Talmudic scholars. Many have argued that the growing reserves would prove a tempting target for a raid, prompting today's retirees to demand more-generous benefits now at the expense of the baby-boom's. But so far, the only raider around has been the spendthrift federal government. Because Congress voted to count each year's Social Security surplus toward the deficit targets of the Gramm-Rudman law, the reserves actually offset a growing portion of the government's ballooning operating deficit. In 1989, for example, the $52 billion Social Security surplus helped mask a large part of the $204 billion deficit in the operating budget. Rather than being used to buy down the national debt and raise national saving, Social Security's cumulative surpluses are effectively being "borrowed" to finance other federal spending.

Moynihan, Heinz and other legislators fought hard in 1989 to strip the reserves out of the Gramm-Rudman calculations and force deeper cuts in the operating deficit. When that effort failed, a disgusted Moynihan turned to a pay-as-you-go plan advocated by former Social Security chief actuary Robert Myers. Under the proposal, benefits for today's and tomorrow's retirees would remain at their currently scheduled levels. But instead of holding steady for the foreseeable future, payroll-tax rates would fall in 1990 and 1991, stay level for the next 25 years and then rise sharply again after 2015. In effect, today's workers would get a tax cut, while tomorrow's workers would pay higher taxes to support baby-boomers when they retire. The reserves would grow only to the point where they constituted a contingency fund to weather recessions equal to about one year's benefits.

Alternative Visions

Most economists lauded Moynihan for focusing attention on government's profligacy and conceded that there was a strong case for returning Social Security to pay as you go. Still, some partisans of the big-reserve buildup criticized Moynihan for abandoning the faith too soon. Henry Aaron of the Brookings Institution contends that a substantial payroll-tax cut now would stimulate too much demand in today's full-employment economy, forcing the Fed to increase interest rates, strengthening the dollar and worsening America's trade deficit. Others pointed out that converting to pay as you go could easily be delayed until 1993 or later, when the system would have a far healthier contingency reserve on hand. And former Social Security Commissioner Robert Ball argues that even if the system returns to pay as you go, Congress shouldn't cut the Social Security portion of the payroll tax but rather transfer some of the revenues to medicare's hospital-insurance trust fund, which faces bankruptcy early in the next decade.

For now, Moynihan has offered no accompanying plan for plugging the extra hole that his proposal would blow in the fiscal 1991 budget. To head off his tax cut, the administration is pushing its own complex, long-term plan to move gradually toward a budget surplus, set up a special fund to reduce the national debt and turn the Social Security reserves into a true stock of national savings. But the merits of such a proposal could ultimately be lost amid widespread public apathy about the deficit. It is clearly possible that Congress could simply vote to slash payroll taxes and swell the budget gap, especially if sluggish economic growth in the current quarter allows it to invoke a provision of the Gramm-Rudman law and suspend the deficit targets.

"Moynihan's plan has at least one other factor in its favor: Many members of America's 21st-century work force aren't around to vote against the higher taxes that his proposal would impose on them."

Moynihan's plan has at least one other factor in its favor: Many members of America's 21st-century work force aren't around to vote against the higher taxes that his proposal would impose on them. With today's workers eager for a break, Capitol Hill could be in for a replay of the 1989 fight over medicare's catastrophic coverage, when lawmakers finally leaped aboard a bandwagon to repeal the program rather than be crushed by it.

Susan Dentzer is a senior editor at U.S. News & World Report, *a weekly newsmagazine.*

"Senator Moynihan's plan to roll back Social Security taxes would . . . return pay-as-you-go honesty to the Social Security system."

Congress Should Adopt the Moynihan Plan

Stephen Moore and Jesse Jackson

Editor's note: The following viewpoint is in two parts. The first part was written by Stephen Moore. The second part was written by Jesse Jackson.

I

By now most Americans have received their first pay checks of 1990. To their shock, their take home pay is smaller than in 1989's final pay check. The reason is the stealth tax hike that is raising Social Security taxes for the seventh time in ten years. This one takes $7 billion out of American pockets, cutting the take-home pay of all American workers by up to $600 a year. As bad, the increased levy on employers will cause many to trim job rolls or cancel their expansion. For 80 percent of middle-income families, the cruelly persistent escalating Social Security taxes have eroded all of their gains from the income tax cuts of the Reagan years.

These tax hikes allegedly are imposed in the name of "saving" the Social Security system. Yet even without the added revenues the retirement program will be financially solvent for at least the next three decades. The new funds, moreover, would not be put aside to build up a reserve to pay out benefits to "baby boomers" when they retire in the next century. Instead, the retirement funds' surplus mountain—$70 billion in 1990 and soaring to $230 billion by the year 2000—are to be spent on current government programs. Nothing is being saved, deposited, or invested for future retirees. "Thievery" is what Senator Daniel Patrick Moynihan, the New York Democrat, correctly brands this and he is attempting to stop it.

As chairman of the Senate Finance Subcommittee on Social Security, Moynihan will introduce legislation to end permanently this congressional mismanagement of Social Security retirement funds

Stephen Moore, "Three Cheers for Moynihan's $55 Billion Tax Cut for Working Americans," The Heritage Foundation *Backgrounder*, January 10, 1990. Reprinted with permission. Jesse Jackson, "Hens Make Out, Hogs Get Slaughtered," *Los Angeles Times*, January 4, 1990. Copyright © 1990, Los Angeles Times. Reprinted with permission.

and grant long overdue tax relief to U.S. wage earners. His plan would cancel 1990's unneeded Social Security payroll tax increase immediately and cut a further 2.2 percentage points in 1991. His intent is to have incoming payroll taxes equal outgoing retirement payments each year. This would give $55 billion back to American workers next year without affecting current or future Social Security benefits. Social Security would become a genuine "pay-as-you-go" system, rather than the cash cow that has been subsidizing federal spending. Moynihan understands the soundness of this. So should George Bush. The President should warmly endorse this tax cut for 120 million American workers. If he does not, he will be making a serious economic (to say nothing of political) mistake.

Since the Social Security program's inception in 1937, when the tax rate was set at two percent of wages for the first $3,000 of earnings, Social Security taxes have risen steadily. In 1960, the taxes amounted to 6 percent of wages; today they are 15.3 percent on income up to $51,300, with half paid directly by workers and half by their employers. The current rate structure was set in 1983 when lawmakers expected sluggish economic growth, and thus low tax receipts, for the remainder of the decade. But the gloomy forecasts proved to be wildly off target. The robust economic expansion of the 1980s, with 18 million new jobs, generated a huge and unexpected surplus in Social Security payroll tax receipts. The Moynihan tax cut proposal merely corrects the tax rates for this error in government forecasting.

Discouraging Hiring

Reducing the payroll tax also would help the American economy enormously. A payroll tax is not merely regressive, falling disproportionately on lower-income workers, but it is one of the most economically destructive ways for the government to raise revenue, because it discourages businesses from hiring additional workers. Former U.S. Treasury economists Aldona and Gary Robbins estimate that the 1988 and 1990 payroll tax hikes will cost Americans 510,000 jobs and reduce gross national product by $320 billion by the year 2000. By contrast, they argue, every dollar reduction in Social Security taxes would expand economic output by 68 cents.

Some critics of the Moynihan plan complain that his reduction in Social Security taxes today would eliminate the surplus needed to pay the benefits when the baby boom generation retires. This ignores one central point: with or without a payroll tax cut, there will be no Social Security fund surplus (actually not even a "fund") since the surplus money routinely is spent on non-Social Security programs as soon as it reaches Washington. All that is in the "fund" is a stack of IOUs from the Treasury. Moving Social Security off budget, as the White House has proposed, would not change this situation. The trust fund still would hold nothing but government IOUs.

"The best way for Congress to protect the solvency of Social Security in the next century is through a pro-growth tax policy."

The best way for Congress to protect the solvency of Social Security in the next century is through a pro-growth tax policy. Part of this is the payroll tax cut recommended by Moynihan. Part of this is the capital gains tax cut urged by Bush. And part could be by other tax reforms, like expanding Individual Retirement Account eligibility. Such a pro-growth tax policy is the best way to assure funds for retiring Americans. Example: If Americans' real per capita incomes were to grow by just 2 percent per year, or about the rate of growth in the 1980s, between 1990 and 2030— the year in which the "baby boom" pressure on Social Security will reach its peak—workers in that year will have more than double the incomes of today's workers. This would substantially ease the burden of paying for retirement and health care programs for the elderly population that year. By contrast, maintaining today's high payroll taxes will dampen productivity and output, meaning tomorrow's workforce will be less capable of paying the bill for retirees.

Controlling the Deficit

Another objection levelled at the Moynihan plan is that a Social Security tax cut will inflate the federal budget deficit. But the regressive Social Security tax was never intended to finance the deficit or pay for any program other than Social Security. Moreover, projections show that with the Moynihan tax cut the deficit can be brought under control through modest spending restraint. For instance, if the Social Security tax were reduced to the level needed just to cover Social Security spending, and all other federal programs were frozen at 1990 levels, the budget would be balanced by 1994.

Thanks to hikes in the Social Security payroll tax, the vast majority of middle-income Americans forfeit a larger share of their income to the federal tax collector in 1990 than they did in 1980. Senator Moynihan's plan to roll back Social Security taxes would end this stealth tax increase and return pay-as-you-go honesty to the Social Security system by preventing Washington from raiding the pension program. The White House should join other champions of economic growth in endorsing the Moynihan tax cut.

II

Among other things, America was founded on the idea of fair taxes. At the Boston Tea Party, we fought a revolution against a system of unjust taxation.

A fair tax is based on the ability to pay. But the current tax system is backward and irrational, filled with illusions and tricks for the unwary. Today, as our tax system's most perceptive critic, multimillionaire Leona Helmsley, told her former housekeeper: "Only the little people pay taxes."

In 1990, Congress faces a crucial test. By passing President Bush's plan to cut taxes for those who have capital and are already making gains, it could return to the dried-up wells of trickle-down economics. This would be a major mistake for the American people.

Alternatively, Congress can move forward to a fair tax policy for all Americans by passing Sen. Daniel Patrick Moynihan's proposal to roll back Social Security taxes. This plan would reduce the tax burden on 110 million working Americans by $55 billion next year and begin to restore fairness to our tax system.

A high Social Security payroll tax is especially unfair because it taxes all employees, whether they are earning $10,000 or $1 million a year, at the same flat rate, now set at 7.65%.

Ham-and-Egg Economics

This George Bush approach is what I call ham-and-egg economics. It looks as if everybody, the hens and the hogs, are contributing equally to make the sandwich. The ham and the eggs, after all, are both between two slices of the same bread. The smell is blended and they are jointly advertised.

But the hens and the hogs are really giving up very different things. While the hen lays an egg and keeps on squawking, the hog gives up a leg and then stops walking. One drop for the hen, a total sacrifice for the hog.

With the Republican ham-and-eggs payroll tax, the hens are making out like bandits while the hogs are getting slaughtered. The unfairness and backwardness of the flat tax is made even worse by the fact that the tax is imposed only on the first $51,300 of wages. This means that someone earning $51,300 a year and someone earning $10 million a year each pay $3,924.

Moynihan's bill is responding to the fact that the revenues from the federal payroll tax, which are supposed to be dedicated to the Social Security trust funds, are in fact being used to pay the general expenses of government.

To correct the misuse of the payroll tax, Moynihan proposes that Congress repeal the recent rate increase and then cut the rate effective Jan. 1, 1991, to 5.1% (6.5% including Medicare). This plan would preserve the integrity of the Social Security system and place it back on the pay-as-you-go basis under which it operated for decades before 1983.

This proposal is fiscally sound and morally right. It is neither sensible nor just to steal from Social Security, which is the solemn promise of one generation to the next, to pay for government services or military technology that we do not have the will to pay for honestly or the courage to do without. The working people of America should not be giving up their hard-earned wages to pay for the government's own fiscal irresponsibility.

Making Up the Deficit

And yet, we cannot stop there. If the Moynihan proposal goes through, we will have to make up the difference between government revenues and expenditures that the Social Security surplus has been used to hide. The Reagan and Bush Administrations have used the trust fund surpluses to mask the true size of the federal deficit. In 1989, for example, President Bush said that the deficit was $152 billion but, without all of the Social Security reserves, it was really a staggering $248 billion. Cutting the capital gains tax now for fewer than 10 million Americans who already have capital, as President Bush proposes, would simply swell the deficit and compound the present irresponsibility.

To bring the deficit down, we need to preserve only necessary military spending and require wealthy Americans and corporations to pay their fair share of taxes. In the 1980s, the Reagan-Bush Administration cut taxes on the wealthy and raised taxes on working- and middle-class families by systematically shifting the tax burden. This was a fraud on the majority of the American people. As Moynihan observed, "The United States almost certainly now has the most regressive tax structure of any Western nation."

A Democratic System

But there are ways to close the gap. We can restore the 1987 income tax rate on the top 600,000 taxpayers to 38.5%. We can impose luxury taxes and a securities transfer excise tax. We can tax corporate polluters, limit the business meals deduction to 50% and close other corporate loopholes. If we combine sensible tax

measures like these with at least a freeze in real military spending, we can stop the destructive cycle of deficit spending.

"To bring the deficit down, we need to preserve only necessary military spending and require wealthy Americans and corporations to pay their fair share of taxes."

We need a new democratic direction for our fiscal policy, and Moynihan's proposal is a step in the right direction. Congress should decide to take a stand with the working people of America and put an end to ham-and-egg economics.

Stephen Moore is a Grover M. Hermann Fellow at the Thomas A. Roe Institute for Economic Policy Studies. As part of The Heritage Foundation in Washington, D.C., the Institute researches economic policy issues. Civil rights leader Jesse Jackson was a 1988 candidate for the Democratic presidential nomination.

viewpoint 23

Congress Should Not Adopt the Moynihan Plan

Robert M. Ball and Warren Brookes

Editor's note: The following viewpoint is in two parts. The first part was written by Robert M. Ball. The second part was written by Warren Brookes.

I

With his proposal to cut $55 billion in Social Security taxes in 1991 alone—more later—Sen. Daniel Patrick Moynihan has turned the long-smoldering dispute over reserve financing for Social Security vs. pay-as-you-go into the hottest argument of the day. He has weighed in on the side of pay-as-you-go, and his views will certainly be listened to with great respect; for over a decade he has been Social Security's leading champion in the Senate.

But is he right? On the matter of pay-as-you-go, my answer is, "Maybe, later on." But on the question of a Social Security tax cut in 1990 or 1991, it is "Absolutely not." Here's why:

1. The old-age, survivors and disability insurance (OASDI) reserve is not yet at a safe level for a pay-as-you-go plan.

Even if we adopt pay-as-you-go, for safety's sake we should not reduce money going into OASDI just yet. In spite of all the talk about a huge reserve accumulating in the trust funds, the buildup lies mostly in the future. The reserves today have not yet reached a contingency level for a pay-as-you-go plan that most experts consider sufficient to protect fully against unexpected adverse economic developments, such as the back-to-back recessions of the late 1970s and early 1980s. Opinions vary, but the majority believe that a fully safe reserve ratio is in the range of 100 percent to 150 percent of the next year's payments. Currently the ratio is 75 percent.

Given the wrenching experience the country went through with two Social Security financial crises, one in the mid-1970s and one in the early 1980s, we ought

Robert M. Ball, "Moynihan's Social Security Bombshell," *The Washington Post National Weekly Edition,* January 29-February 4, 1990. © 1990 by The Washington Post. Warren Brookes, "Real Reform for Social Security," *The Washington Times,* February 1, 1990. Reprinted by permission of Warren Brookes and Creators Syndicate.

to make certain that the contingency reserve provides a substantial cushion. I would favor keeping the reserve at a ratio of 150 percent. This level will not be reached until sometime between 1993 and 1995, depending on economic performance.

2. The Medicare program is underfinanced.

Medicare's hospital insurance program, which is paid for by part of the Social Security tax, is clearly underfinanced, with only 1.45 percent of covered earnings allocated to it out of the overall Social Security contribution rate of 7.65 percent. The best guess is that if the economy performs less well than it has in the recent past, payments from hospital insurance could start to exceed income as early as 1995, with all the bonds held in the hospital insurance fund liquidated by the end of the decade.

Transferring Funds

If we decide to adopt pay-as-you-go for Social Security, the safe way to do it is to transfer part of the OASDI rate over to Medicare, just as in the past the tax rate has been reallocated between old-age and survivors insurance and disability insurance. Otherwise we will cut the combined rate now with great fanfare and just have to raise it again for Medicare's sake very soon—unless, of course, it is decided to cut benefits. That is always a possibility if the programs get close to the financial cliff, as OASDI did in 1982. That financing crisis was resolved by benefit cuts in the 1983 amendments along with tax increases. The best protection for benefit levels in both OASDI and Medicare is adequate financing.

A good pay-as-you-go plan would be to wait until 1995, when an adequate contingency reserve is ensured, and then transfer from OASDI to Medicare the part of the OASDI rate now being proposed as a cut. Medicare would then be fully financed for the next 25 years and would end the period with a reasonable contingency reserve. Given the high degree of uncertainty about health care arrangements beyond 25 years, that would seem to be long enough to provide for Medicare financing.

A pay-as-you go plan would, of course, call for lower taxes now than a reserve plan, and higher taxes later. Without taking into account the clear need to increase Medicare rates during the period, the OASDI rates could be lower than the present 6.2 percent for 25 years, but then would have to rise well above that level by 2020. Under present law or pay-as-you-go, the rate will have to rise to around 8 percent from the middle of the next century on.

3. Dropping the other shoe: What happens after a Social Security tax cut?

Middle-income workers better not start spending the money—up to $600—being promised from a Social Security tax cut. To avoid increases in the deficit, a Social Security tax cut could/would most likely be followed by increases in general taxes large enough to make up for both the employee rate reduction and the employer reduction. With deficits as high as they are, and with many unmet needs that only government can meet, it is unrealistic to think that one source of government revenue can be cut without another being raised.

4. The longer-range issue: Reserve financing vs. pay-as-you-go.

What about the longer-range issue of returning Social Security funding to pay-as-you-go? Here I say, "Maybe." The answer depends largely on whether a fund buildup would be handled so as to increase national saving, or whether government borrowing from the fund would just substitute for general taxes or pay for the current expenditures of new or bigger programs.

The Problem of Productivity

Since the retirees of the future have to be supported out of the goods and services produced in the future, the only present actions that can help meet their needs are those that improve our capacity to produce. If the buildup of reserves results in a greater surplus in the total accounts of the government, then the Social Security reserves increase national saving and the capacity to produce goods and service.

On the other hand, if a surplus merely substitutes for higher general taxes or supports a greater level of expenditures, the Social Security buildup does not contribute to economic growth, and paying Social Security claims will be as much of a burden as under pay-as-you-go.

A Social Security buildup that increases our capacity to produce is theoretically possible but not easy to accomplish. The political system has to exercise enough restraint to finance programs other than Social Security without relying on borrowing from the trust funds. In spite of his past support for accumulating reserves, Sen. Moynihan has evidently become discouraged about reserve financing, and believes now that a buildup in the funds would

simply hold down general taxes. If he is correct that we do not have the discipline to keep from borrowing Social Security funds to pay for the increases in the current operating expenses of government, then once the OASDI funds reach an adequate contingency level, we should stop the buildup and shift part of the tax rate to Medicare.

II

If Sen. Daniel Patrick Moynihan, New York Democrat, were really interested in reforming Social Security financing and helping the middle class, he wouldn't be acting like the bordello piano player who pretends not to know what is going on upstairs.

When he voted to raise Social Security taxes in 1983 and deliberately generate a "surplus," Mr. Moynihan surely knew that, by law, Social Security trust funds could only be invested in federal debt. Therefore, they had to wind up being spent to reduce the federal deficit.

That he should now express surprise, indignation and even outrage this is happening, is at the very least disingenuous.

Maybe he hopes we'll forget that, from 1965 to 1972, Lyndon Johnson and Mr. Moynihan's old boss, Richard Nixon, quietly used $17.1 billion in Social Security surpluses to finance the Vietnam War and cut total deficits of those years from $61.7 billion to $44.6 billion.

Worse, when he was confronted by Office of Management and Budget Director Richard Darman, it was clear Mr. Moynihan had no idea how he would deal either with the revenue loss of $55 billion a year or the much more serious question of financing the massive benefit spike 20 years from now, when payroll tax rates would have to soar.

This suggests Mr. Moynihan's whole move was, as the White House charged, nothing more than a political gimmick to stop the Bush capital-gains tax cut, not a solution for a very real problem.

"Since the retirees of the future have to be supported out of the goods and services produced in the future, the only present actions that can help meet their needs are those that improve our capacity to produce."

That suspicion was reinforced when he quickly trashed the plan designed by Rep. John Porter, Illinois Republican, to which President Bush gave only tentative and cautious support.

Mr. Porter's plan calls for giving the surplus Social Security taxes back to taxpayers who deposit them in bonded, private *individual* tax-free retirement accounts. In return, their future Social Security benefits are reduced, dollar for dollar. The surplus rebate starts out at 1.9 percent of wages and rises to nearly 3 percent (counting employer and employee taxes).

Mr. Porter is still waiting for a General Accounting Office study of the economics of his proposal, but an analysis developed by economists at the U.S. Chamber of Commerce shows that the individual retiring in 2018 will have generated a tax-free account of as much as $73,000 at current Treasury bill rates (7.8 percent).

That may not sound like much, but by requiring that those funds be used to pay benefits first, it effectively postpones the time when the retiree uses full Social Security benefits. That would keep the Social Security system cash flow solvent— that is, able to meet all current benefit demands out of current payroll tax revenues until the year 2046 or 28 years beyond the present projected deficit point of 2018.

Mr. Moynihan characterized this as "dismantling Social Security," but Mr. Porter told us, "If anything, he's the one doing the dismantling. With his plan of cutting taxes, he will surely force the cutting of benefits, unless he provides some way to deal with the baby-boom retirees."

The Darman Proposal

But what about the Darman proposal to use the Social Security reserves to reduce the federal public debt? "I don't think anybody in America really believes that Congress will allow $3 trillion to accumulate that way without touching it," Mr. Porter said.

"If you look back in the 1960s when the Social Security trust funds were really flush, we immediately created Medicare, Supplemental Security Income and disability, and the system was broke by 1973, again in 1977, and again in 1983."

But why not do as Mr. Moynihan says and simply go back to a full "pay as you go" plan? Mr. Porter said: "When the baby boomers retire in the next century, there won't be enough workers to take care of them. We have three workers for every retiree now; by 2030, we could be down to 1.5. When that happens, pay-as-you-go will fail us.

"We have to find a way to put the reserve out of the reach of future Congresses to spend but make it still available to provide retirement benefits. Sen. Moynihan's plan does the first but not the second."

But isn't Mr. Porter's plan really a back door to the privatization of Social Security? "I don't deny I would very much like to see a vested, fully funded Social Security system that is not in the hands of the politicians but is in the hands of the American worker."

When Mr. Porter's plan was first outlined to the president, Mr. Bush was enthusiastic about the huge impact this could have on raising the domestic savings rate by as much as 3 percentage points, providing a very strong, supply-side boost to the economy.

Why then is the White House still so skittish? They remember 1982, when Democrats slaughtered Republicans for even discussing Social Security reform. But Mr. Porter told us, "We have had too much Social Security politics, too much cheap demagoguery. The American workers deserve better."

"We have had too much Social Security politics, too much cheap demagoguery. The American workers deserve better."

In a way, Mr. Moynihan has given Republicans like Mr. Porter cover to talk about reform: "He's done two wonderful things: Put the issue on the table and blown the whistle on the way we are blowing away our children's retirement funds now. His diagnosis was dead right, his prescription is pure poison."

Robert M. Ball was Social Security Commissioner from 1962 to 1974. He also served as a Democratic representative on the National Commission on Social Security Reform from 1982 to 1983. Warren Brookes is a nationally syndicated columnist who writes about economic issues.

viewpoint 24

Individual Retirement Accounts Should Replace Social Security

John Porter and Paul Craig Roberts

Editor's note: The following viewpoint is in two parts. The first part was written by John Porter. The second part was written by Paul Craig Roberts.

I

The 1983 Social Security amendments raised payroll taxes gradually but substantially to create a $3 trillion (in current dollars) reserve by the 2020s. A reserve of this magnitude will be needed to provide for the retirement of the "baby boomers," when there will be relatively fewer workers and more retirees.

What are we going to do with this $3 trillion? Currently, two bad ideas are on the table—the first is to cut the tax rate and gut the trust fund; the second is to retain the status quo by pouring the growing reserve into Treasury debt. There is a better way: Congress and the president should move now to begin the transformation of Social Security into vested, funded, worker-owned retirement accounts.

Gobbling Up Taxes

The time is ripe for action because the reserve is now accumulating. Some $58 billion was added in 1989, $65 billion in 1990 and larger amounts are coming each year in the future. But because the Social Security reserve must by law be invested in U.S. government obligations, these funds are being consumed to cover general revenue deficits. Cutting the Social Security tax, although it would stop the deficit from gobbling up Social Security tax payments, would also end the accumulation of the needed retirement reserve. A Social Security tax cut would therefore require either large tax increases or substantial benefit cuts later on.

To prevent Congress from spending the reserve and to preserve it for retirement benefits, the U.S. should refund each and every year the total amount of Social

John Porter, "Let Workers Own Their Retirement Funds," *The Wall Street Journal*, February 1, 1990. Reprinted with permission of The Wall Street Journal © 1990 Dow Jones & Company, Inc. All rights reserved. Paul Craig Roberts, "Sliding Social Security," *The Washington Times*, January 2, 1990. Reprinted with permission.

Security taxes not needed for current benefits into Individual Social Security Retirement Accounts for every U.S. worker. The government would adjust the worker's claim on the Social Security reserve to reflect the amount of his or her retirement income that would come from his or her ISSRA.

This plan would clearly take decades of transition, during which a greater and greater percentage of each worker's Social Security taxes would be diverted to an ISSRA, and a falling proportion would remain in the current trust fund. Today's 60-year-old worker would receive most of his retirement benefits from the trust fund, and only a small portion from his ISSRA. By contrast, a child born today would receive all of his government mandated benefits from an ISSRA.

Each worker would own this account, invest and reinvest it over his working lifetime, and upon reaching retirement age would buy a lifetime annuity that, history tells us, would provide a far more generous retirement benefit than is currently provided by Social Security.

These retirement accounts would be held for their owners by qualified, bonded Social Security trustees—banks, insurance companies, brokers and other money managers—and invested according to safe fiduciary standards in federal, state and local government obligations, time deposits, corporate AAA bonds, certain mutual funds and similar non-speculative investments. Trustees would be required by law to follow the investment standards and to pay the fund to the owner only when he or she reaches retirement age—early withdrawals for any purpose would be prohibited. Neither the amounts refunded nor the earnings on such ISSRA accounts would be subject to income taxes, and the ISSRA would become part of the individual's estate upon death.

Under such a system, approximately $60 billion would be refunded into 130 million Individual Social Security Retirement Accounts in 1990. The amounts in following years would be even larger. Individuals could count on their Social Security taxes being there for them on retirement—a certainty they do not enjoy now, when the money is at the mercy of Congress's spending proclivities. And because the vested funds would yield a higher rate of return than monies placed by the Social Security Administration in Treasury debt, the long-term unfunded liabilities of the government's retirement system would be substantially mitigated.

For an 18-year-old entering the workforce in 1990 and retiring in 2039, the proportion of his annual contributions to Social Security that is not needed by present retirees is one-sixth, or $27,000 over his working lifetime. That amount would be rebated to his ISSRA every year. By investing this annual rebate conservatively and realizing a 3.6% real interest rate, this worker would create an ISSRA nest egg of $61,578 (again, in 1990 dollars) by retirement. This amount would be in addition to his adjusted claim on the regular Social Security Trust Fund.

By comparison, that same $27,000 kept in the current Social Security Trust Fund would be invested in Treasury debt yielding around 2% in real terms. This interest increment must inevitably be paid by other direct or indirect taxes on the American workforce of the future.

By transferring their retirement money to ISSRAs, today's young workers would be guaranteed security in their senior years while the stress on the trust fund would be greatly alleviated. Gradually, over a 50-year period, the U.S. would move from the present unvested, unfunded system, subject to the whims of Congress, to a fully vested, fully funded system owned by the beneficiaries.

The effects on the American economy would be profound. A substantial base of domestic savings and investment would be created and would help end our heavy dependence on foreign capital. These investments would drive down interest rates and encourage economic expansion. Every American worker, many of whom have never been able to save, would have a direct financial stake in the success of the U.S. economy.

Mask Deficits

The White House and the Congress, as well as the leadership of both parties, have acknowledged that use of the Social Security reserve to mask general account deficits must cease. But even if Social Security were removed from budgetary and Gramm-Rudman calculations, it is extremely doubtful that future Congresses would allow a $3 trillion reserve to accumulate untouched.

This growing reserve must be used as the point of departure to create a Social Security system for the next century that will protect American workers and strengthen our nation's economy. The opportunity is at hand. It should not be allowed to pass.

II

The 1980s are justly known as the Reagan decade to honor the man who re-established the right of every American to be the majority shareholder in his own income. To whom will the 1990s belong? The decade may belong to the person who stops the long slide of Social Security into welfarism by establishing a sound pension basis for the system.

Such a person faces a big challenge, as Jan. 1, 1990, brought dismal developments on the Social Security front. First the combined payroll tax rate rose from 15.02 percent to 15.30 percent, adding $62 to the competitive disadvantage of goods and services produced by the average U.S. worker.

Second, the maximum wage and salary base against which the payroll tax is applied rose from $48,000 to $51,300 adding $144 to the competitive disadvantage of goods and services produced by higher-paid Americans.

Third, the increase in the payroll tax base was calculated, for the first time, by including 401K retirement plans, thus opening the door for taxation of private pension plans to pay for Social Security benefits.

"Even if Social Security were removed from budgetary and Gramm-Rudman calculations, it is extremely doubtful that future Congresses would allow a $3 trillion reserve to accumulate untouched."

Fourth, 1990 is the year during which Congress plans to take Social Security off budget, where surplus revenues will disappear in a variety of back-room bailouts.

Congress, of course, will claim it is taking Social Security off budget to protect the "trust funds" from being spent to cover the government's annual budget deficits. But once off budget, the surplus Social Security revenues will be spent in even less desirable ways to benefit a variety of special interests. The following are among the likely uses of off-budget "trust-fund" revenues:

• They will be "invested" in state and local municipal bonds "to rebuild our infrastructure," thereby allowing the secretary of the treasury to buy elections for the party in power.

• They will be "invested" in securities issued to bail out Third World debtors and their creditors.

• They will be "invested" in securities issued in the $200 billion savings and loan bailout.

• They will be "invested" in securities issued to bail out junk bond defaults "in order to save jobs and prevent foreigners from buying up America."

All of these "securities" will consist of taxpayer-guaranteed government IOUs. In other words, nothing real will be in the "trust fund," but Congress will have been spared a lot of political headaches by having a ready cache of money available.

The "trust fund" will show holdings of "guaranteed" securities, and all of the accounting will be legal. Nevertheless, a scam will have been perpetrated, and the "trust fund" will consist of nothing but the government's ability to raise taxes to redeem its IOUs.

A Collective Fund Is Impossible

It is madness to believe that there can be a collective Social Security trust fund. In the first place, there are no real investments in which to place such large sums of money without socializing American industry. If the surplus revenues predicted for the next 20 years materialize and are used to purchase corporate stocks and bonds, control over U.S. business will pass to the trustees of the Social Security trust fund.

If the revenues are invested in U.S. government bonds, the money will continue to be used to finance the government's annual budget. If the revenues are used to pay down the national debt, the result will be to use payroll tax receipts to create capital gains for existing bond holders (by driving up the price of bonds) and to subsidize the treasury's borrowing cost (by driving down the interest rate). These are not valid uses of taxes on American labor.

Unless the trust fund is kept in the form of accumulating cash balances in the banking system, which is highly unlikely, there is no other use for Social Security trust fund revenues except to purchase "securities" issued to benefit a variety of special interests.

"Once part of Social Security is privatized in the form of individually held trust funds, the public quickly will realize the superiority of this approach."

The way to create a real Social Security trust fund is to refund the surplus revenues for investment in Individual Retirement Accounts. Then the revenues can be invested in income-producing assets, such as corporate stocks and bonds, without jeopardizing our free enterprise system.

Moreover, this removes a portion of Social Security benefits from the backs of future taxpayers and allows a corresponding reduction in the benefits payable by the government.

Once part of Social Security is privatized in the form of individually held trust funds, the public quickly will realize the superiority of this approach. The individual trust funds would be inheritable, thus allowing the buildup of private wealth—something the existing Social Security system cannot accomplish.

And, since the trust funds would be funded privately, we would escape the risk of having the government eventually pay our Social Security pension by taxing our private pension.

Rep. John Porter, Republican of Illinois, wants to stop the government from spending our Social Security taxes. He also wants to prevent the government from using Social Security revenues to bail out special interests. The only way this can be done is the way he proposes to do it: Put the surplus Social Security revenues in Individual Retirement Accounts, where the government can't get its hands on them.

If the 1990s become known as the "Porter Decade," we all will have reason to cheer.

John Porter is a Republican representative from Illinois. He is a member of the House Appropriations Committee and the House Select Committee on Aging. Paul Craig Roberts is an economist at the Center for Strategic and International Studies in Washington, D.C., and a columnist for The Washington Times.

"Privatization schemes may provide certain advantages to high-income, steady workers. . . . For the majority of workers, however, Social Security is often better."

Individual Retirement Accounts Should Not Replace Social Security

Bruce D. Schobel

In recent weeks, several proposals to modify the financing of the Social Security program have been widely described and discussed. The opening shot in this debate was fired by Sen. Daniel Patrick Moynihan, who proposed adjusting the payroll tax rate to eliminate the surpluses that are building up. Sen. Moynihan's payroll-tax rates would be lower than those scheduled in present law from 1990 until the year 2014, the same as the present rates in 2015-19 and higher in 2020 and after. His proposal is financially sound and would restore the program's long-range actuarial balance, which has been steadily deteriorating since 1983. The proposal does little, however, to create the additional national savings that will be necessary to finance the retirement of the baby boom generation.

Rep. John Porter (R., Ill.) has suggested an alternative proposal. His plan would slowly, over a 50-year period, privatize Social Security, replacing the existing government program with Individual Social Security Retirement Accounts (ISSRAs). During the long transition period, workers who voluntarily contribute to ISSRAs would forgo a pro rata share of the Social Security benefits they would have earned if those contributions had been paid to Social Security. The Porter proposal is the end result of a decade of evolution and refinement of annuity-type privatization proposals and is much more difficult to evaluate than the simple Moynihan proposal.

Proposals for Reform

The seminal work on annuity-type privatization schemes was done in the late 1970s by Michael Boskin, now chairman of the President's Council of Economic Advisers, and three colleagues. They wrote a paper for the National Federation of Independent Business (NFIB) describing how Social Security's

"transfer" and "annuity" components could be separated. The transfer function would remain the province of the government; the annuity function would be privatized. This early proposal got little attention.

In 1981, the Reagan administration arrived on the scene. It was expected to be receptive to privatization of Social Security, and no less than three serious proposals were presented for consideration in that first year. One came from Ralph Saul, then chairman of INA Corp., a large insurance company, now part of CIGNA; another, from the NFIB, was based on the work done for it earlier by Mr. Boskin; the third came from Peter Ferrara, later a White House policy adviser and now a law professor. The Ferrara proposal, which was the most fully developed, was also based largely on Mr. Boskin's work. I was involved in analyzing these proposals while at the Social Security Administration. All had shortcomings; none was found by the administration to be worthy of further development.

In August 1982, Mr. Boskin presented a new version of his proposal, renamed "Personal Security Accounts," to the National Commission on Social Security—the Greenspan Commission—through the use of "Super-IRAs." Although the new proposal was much improved, it was not seriously considered by the Reagan administration and it soon disappeared.

All of the privatization schemes of the early 1980s offered workers financial incentives to switch their contributions voluntarily from Social Security to the new private accounts. The most extreme example was the 1984 Ferrara proposal, which provided 100% tax credits to workers who switched to Super-IRAs; they would, in effect, be investing the Treasury's money! These financial incentives were enormously expensive—one major reason the proposals were never seriously considered.

The Porter proposal is the culmination of this decade of development. It has none of the obvious flaws of the early proposals. It drops the financial incentives, which have become less necessary as Social Security's costs have risen. Although Mr. Boskin, the spiritual godfather of the Porter plan, doesn't discuss Social Security much in his new position, his influence is discernible in the comments of President Bush, who said that the Porter plan has "interesting ingredients." Has Rep. Porter presented a plan that should be enacted into law?

No, not in my opinion. The most fundamental problems with all privatization schemes, including Rep. Porter's, cannot be fixed. First, they remove the "weighting" of the present Social Security benefit formula, which provides higher rates of return to low-income workers than to high-income ones. This shifting of resources from rich to poor, which incidentally mitigates the supposed "regressive" nature of the payroll tax, keeps millions of elderly and disabled people off the welfare rolls. The hidden costs of expanded welfare benefits after privatization of Social Security cannot be ignored.

"Social Security protects the retirement benefit by providing five 'drop-out years'; with the privatization schemes, future benefits would be lost."

Second, the inevitable benefit comparisons between Social Security and the private schemes are very misleading. They always assume very high real rates of return, as high as 12% in some of the early versions. Rep. Porter illustrates the benefits of his proposal with a 3.6% real rate of return, but even this rate is probably not sustainable over the very long time periods that must be considered. After all, if investors could earn interest forever at a rate higher than the real GNP [gross national product] growth, they would be well-advised to liquidate all their investments and simply put their money into these IRAs.

The benefit comparisons also assume steady lifetime earnings—and contributions. Real workers often have periods of unemployment (for child-raising, for instance), or reduced earnings for other reasons. In those cases, Social Security protects the retirement benefit by providing five "drop-out years"; with the privatization schemes, future benefits would be lost. Last but not least, Social Security benefits are indexed to the cost of living: The benefits from IRAs are not and cannot be indexed. Thus, while the initial benefits may be comparable, the private benefit can be expected to fall further and further behind Social Security as time goes by.

Third, IRA-type benefits are often inadequate for the disabled or for survivors because workers have not always had time to accumulate significant account

balances. This problem does not arise under Social Security, of course.

Privatization schemes may provide certain advantages to high-income, steady workers who are never unemployed and do not become disabled or die young. For the majority of workers, however, Social Security is often better. If Social Security were privatized, the demands on the government to provide supplemental benefits in many cases would be irresistible, and these benefits would be expensive.

I am not suggesting that all is well with Social Security and that it should be left unchanged. In 1988, before most politicians were willing to discuss needed changes in Social Security openly, former Deputy Social Security Commissioner Enid Borden and I developed a proposal that embodied the best parts of the recent proposals by Sen. Moynihan and by Rep. Porter. It deserves serious consideration today.

The Borden-Schobel solution would finance the Social Security program on a pay-as-you-go basis, transferring to it only those payroll-tax collections that are needed immediately to pay benefits and administrative costs. The additional payroll taxes that Social Security does not need to pay present deposits would be deposited in IRA-type accounts in approved financial institutions chosen by workers themselves. The benefits from these accounts would supplement Social Security, but Social Security benefits would not be affected. The amounts deposited in the private accounts would be about $40 billion in 1990 alone, increasing gradually to about $160 billion in 2010, after which the annual amounts would decline. Even if the private accounts earned interest at only the same rate as the Social Security trust fund, the total amount held on deposit would be roughly $5 trillion in 2015, or about $2 trillion in 1990 dollars.

Like the Moynihan and Porter proposals, ours would pump into the Social Security program only enough funds to pay current expenses. Like Rep. Porter, we would establish private IRA-type investment accounts into which workers would deposit excess payroll taxes; unlike Rep. Porter, we would make these deposits mandatory, not voluntary. Like Sen. Moynihan, and unlike Rep. Porter, we would not reduce Social Security benefits.

Rep. Porter would reduce future benefits in proportion to the contributions made in his ISSRAs. For example, a worker who contributes to an ISSRA one-tenth of his or her payroll taxes for a year would forgo one-tenth of the Social Security benefits attributable to that year's earnings. (The precise calculation has not been explained.)

Enid Borden and I reject these benefit reductions because they imply that the present relationship between taxes and benefits is exactly correct. In our view, the benefit structure is not the problem; the taxes are. We would divert the excess taxes into productive investments, but we see no reason to penalize workers for saving these additional amounts.

Rep. Porter would make workers hit a moving target: With every dollar a worker saves in an ISSRA, he or she would lose some Social Security benefits, thereby requiring more savings, which would trigger more benefit reductions, etc.

Net Savings

In evaluating the net savings that may result from any of the current proposals, the most important short-term consideration is how the government will react. If it borrows on the open market the same amount that it used to obtain from Social Security, we will have higher interest rates, no net savings, and other negative effects. Of course, the likelihood is that government spending would be reduced somewhat, thereby reducing the government's need to borrow. Eventually, the deficit problems may be solved.

Even if the budget deficit were eliminated, the Moynihan proposal cannot be expected to produce as much savings as the IRA-type proposals would produce. The Porter plan, however, would accompany its savings with benefit cuts, increasing the future needs that it is trying to finance. The Borden-Schobel plan would save all of the excess payroll taxes and accumulate tremendous private savings, without cutting Social Security benefits.

"Even if the budget deficit were eliminated, the Moynihan proposal cannot be expected to produce as much savings as the IRA-type proposals would produce."

In any case, we need to look beyond the paper-shuffling of artificial government trust funds to the economic reality of meeting the future retirement needs of the baby boomers. The only long-term solution is to create additional national savings and invest those savings in ways that will increase the productivity of future workers.

Bruce D. Schobel was an actuary and policy adviser at the Social Security Administration from 1979 to 1988.

bibliography

The following bibliography of books, periodicals,
and pamphlets is divided into chapter topics
for the reader's convenience.

The Budget Deficit

Robert L. Bartley et al.	"The Great Deficit Debate," *National Review*, January 27, 1989.
C. Fred Bergsten	"Attacking the Deficits Now Will Bring Years of Prosperity," *Fortune*, January 2, 1989.
Alan S. Blinder	"Getting Back to the Spirit of Gramm-Rudman," *Business Week*, October 30, 1989.
Alan S. Blinder	"Is the Deficit Too High? Yes. Should It Be Higher? Maybe," *Business Week*, February 20, 1989.
Robert J. Bresler	"Bush and the Deficit Dilemma," *USA Today*, May 1989.
Warren Brookes	"Deficit May Hold Back Liberal Spenders," *Conservative Chronicle*, January 24, 1990. Available from *Conservative Chronicle*, Box 11297, Des Moines, IA 50340-1297
Vivian Brownstein	"In the Budget Battle, There's Not Much Room to Maneuver," *Fortune*, February 26, 1990.
Margaret Carlson	"Déjà Voodoo?" *Time*, March 26, 1990.
Lindley H. Clark Jr.	"Budget Restraint—If Not Now, Maybe Never," *The Wall Street Journal*, February 2, 1990.
The Congressional Digest	"Balanced Budget Constitutional Amendment: Pro & Con," November 1989.
Christopher Cox	"Tame the Budget Beast," *Conservative Digest*, July/August 1989.
James A. Dorn and William A. Niskansen	*Dollars, Deficits, and Trade.* Norwell, MA: Kluwer Academic Publishers, 1989.
Howard Gleckman	"The Bottom Line: Gramm-Rudman Isn't Working," *Business Week*, April 10, 1989.
J. Peter Grace	"The Deficit Time Bomb," *Vital Speeches of the Day*, April 15, 1989.
Robert L. Heilbroner	"All Rich Nations Need Their Debt," *The Nation*, January 23, 1989.
Robert L Heilbroner and Peter Bernstein	*The Debt and the Deficit: False Alarms/ Real Possibilities.* New York: W.W. Norton and Co., 1989.
Robert Kuttner	"Bad Politics, but Worse Economics," *Los Angeles Times*, March 18, 1990.
Robert Kuttner	"The Fudge Factor," *The New Republic*, June 19, 1989.
Thomas E. Mann and Charles L. Schultze	"How to End the Budget Deficit," *The World & I*, January 1989.
Stephen Moore	*Slashing the Deficit: Fiscal Year 1990.* Washington, DC: The Heritage Foundation, 1989.
Alan Murray	"The Budget Albatross," *The Wall Street Journal*, January 20, 1989.
The New Republic	"Bring Back Big Spending," March 27, 1989.
Marshall Robinson	"America's Not-So-Troubling Debts and Deficits," *Harvard Business Review*, July/August 1989.
Isabel V. Sawhill	"Don't Mess With Gramm-Rudman," *The New York Times*, October 22, 1989.
Jeff A. Schnepper	"Social Security and the Budget Deficit," *USA Today*, January 1990.
Leonard Silk	"A New Warning on the Deficits," *The New York Times*, May 5, 1989.
Herbert Stein	"Moynihan Lays Budget Debate Bare," *The Wall Street Journal*, January 24, 1990.
John E. Yang	"Ever-Growing Deficits Establish the Failure of Gramm-Rudman," *The Wall Street Journal*, October 3, 1989.

Social Security

Henry J. Aaron, Barry P. Bosworth, and Gary T. Burtless	*Can America Afford to Grow Old?: Paying for Social Security.* Washington, DC: The Brookings Institution, 1989.
Jeffrey Bell	"Moynihan Plan? A Good Idea, Even If Stolen," *The Wall Street Journal*, February 26, 1990.
Paul Blustein	"The Flap over Social Security," *The Washington Post National Weekly Edition*, January 22-28, 1990.
Warren Brookes	"Cut the Social Security Payroll Tax," *Conservative Chronicle*, January 24, 1990. Available from *Conservative Chronicle*, Box 11297, Des Moines, IA 50340-1297.
Marth Derthick	*Agency Under Stress: The Social Security Administration in American Government.* Washington, DC: The Brookings Institution, 1990.
Stephen J. Entin	"Moynihan Is Right—Now, Cut Benefits," *The Wall Street Journal*, January 29, 1990.
Paul A. Gigot	"Moynihan's Plan: It's Sneaky, but He Has a Point," *The Wall Street Journal*, January 26, 1990.

Howard Gleckman — "Social Security's Dirty Little Secret," *Business Week*, January 29, 1990.

Dan Goodgame — "Read Those Lips: More Taxes," *Time*, January 22, 1990.

Mickey Kaus — "Watch What You Call Welfare," *The Washington Monthly*, March 1989.

Michael Kinsley — "A Liberal Tax Cut," *The New Republic*, January 8 & 15, 1990.

Richard Lacayo — "Dirty Little Secret," *Time*, February 19, 1990.

Paul W. McCracken — "Social Security: Just Another Handout," *The Wall Street Journal*, February 5, 1990.

Colleen McGuiness — *Aging in America: The Federal Government's Role*. Washington, DC: Congressional Quarterly Inc., 1989.

William McGurn — "Fumbling on Social Security," *National Review*, February 19, 1990.

Daniel J. Mitchell — "Cut the Social Security Payroll Tax," *Policy Analysis*, March 8, 1990. Available from Cato Institute, 224 Second St. SE, Washington, DC 20003.

David Moberg — "Sen. Moynihan's Proposal Sparks Social Insecurity," *In These Times*, February 14-20, 1990.

William Murchison — "We Need Radical Reform, Not Tax Increases," *Conservative Chronicle*, February 7, 1990. Available from *Conservative Chronicle*, Box 11297, Des Moines, IA 50340-1297.

The New Republic — "Read His Lips," February 12, 1990.

Paul Craig Roberts — "It's High Time We Retired the Social Security Tax Surplus," *Business Week*, January 15, 1990.

Taxes

Henry Aaron — "If U.S. Is Unequal, Don't Blame the Payroll Tax," *The Wall Street Journal*, February 14, 1990.

Howard Banks — "A Liberal Embraces the Supply-Side," *Forbes*, March 5, 1990.

Fred Barnes — "Unkindest Cut," *The New Republic*, February 5, 1990.

Paul Blustein — "Will a Capital Gains Tax Cut Open a Pandora's Box?" *The Washington Post National Weekly Edition*, March 6-12, 1989.

Bill Bradley — "Capital Gains: Breaking the Compact," *The Washington Post National Weekly Edition*, October 2-8, 1989.

Lindley H. Clark Jr. — "Maybe the Bush Capital-Gains Plan Isn't Enough," *The Wall Street Journal*, February 16, 1990.

Congressional Digest — "Capital Gains Tax: Pro & Con," January 1990.

Susan Dentzer — "The People Tax Reform Left Behind," *U.S. News & World Report*, April 17, 1989.

Jack Egan — "Capitol Pains on Capital Gains," *U.S. News & World Report*, August 7, 1989.

Christopher Farrell — "Learning to Kick the Debt Habit," *Business Week*, March 12, 1990.

Bruce L. Fisher — "Bush Crowd Has a Plan for Broad Tax Retreat: Bite Will Be on Middle and Lower Class," *Los Angeles Times*, October 2, 1989.

James K. Galbraith — *Balancing Acts: Technology, Finance, and the American Future*. New York: Basic Books, 1989.

James K. Galbraith — "Be a Man, Congress—Raise Taxes," *The Wall Street Journal*, September 14, 1989.

Howard Gleckman — "A Tax Break Geared to High Rollers," *Business Week*, August 14, 1989.

Howard Gleckman — "Tinkering with Tax Reform: A Bad Idea that Will Just Get Worse," *Business Week*, November 6, 1989.

The Heritage Foundation — "Taxes, Economic Growth, and Budget Deficits: What Washington Can Learn from the States," The Heritage Foundation *State Backgrounder*, February 9, 1990. Available from The Heritage Foundation, 214 Massachusetts Ave. NE, Washington, DC 20002.

Ernest F. Hollings — "Decaying America: The Underside of the Reagan Legacy," *The Washington Post National Weekly Edition*, March 8-14, 1989.

Mark D. Isaacs — "The Social Security Sinkhole," *The New American*, February 26, 1990.

Robert Kasten — "The Conservative Case for Cutting Payroll Taxes," *The Heritage Lectures*, February 22, 1990. Available from The Heritage Foundation, 214 Massachusetts Ave. NE, Washington, DC 20002.

David Kirkpatrick — "CEOs to Bush: Raise Taxes Now," *Fortune*, January 16, 1989.

Robert Kuttner — "The Trickle-Up Effect of a Capital-Gains Tax Cut," *Business Week*, August 14, 1989.

Lawrence B. Lindsey — "It's Time for Another Cut in Tax Rates, *Forbes*, March 5, 1990.

David Moberg — "Capital Gains Tax Break: Handout for the Least Deserving," *In These Times*, October 25-31, 1989.

Ralph Nader — "Corporate Welfare State Is on a Roll," *Los Angeles Times*, March 5, 1990.

The New Republic — "Them's the Breaks," February 12, 1990.

Don J. Pease — "Back into the Thicket with Bush," *Los Angeles Times*, February 1, 1989.

Joseph A. Pecham — *Tax Reform: The Rich and the Poor*. Washington, DC: The Brookings Institution, 1989.

John B. Shoven — *Debt, Taxes, and Corporate Restructuring*. Washington, DC: The Brookings Institution, 1990.

Herbert Stein — "Common Sense on Capital Gains," *The Wall Street Journal*, August 23, 1989.

John A. Tatom — "Capital Gains Tax: Lower Is Fairer and More Efficient," *The Wall Street Journal*, June 14, 1989.

James Tobin — "How Cutting Taxation Is Just Misrepresentation," *The Washington Post National Weekly Edition*, January 29-February 4, 1990.

Jude Wanniski — "To Aid the Poor, Cut Capital Gains Taxes," *The New York Times*, July 25, 1989.

Trade

Brian Ahlberg — "Trade: Major Political Issue of the 1990s?" *Utne Reader*, November/December 1989.

Norm Alster — "Unlevel Playing Field," *Forbes,* June 26, 1989.

William T. Archey — "Super 301: Just Claiming Our Rights," *The Wall Street Journal,* June 22, 1989.

Paul Blustein — "Looking Overseas to Save the American Economy," *The Washington Post National Weekly Edition,* December 18-24, 1989.

Lindley H. Clark Jr. — "Our Do-It-Yourself Trade Policy," *The Wall Street Journal,* September 22, 1989.

Jean Cobb — "Political Currency," *Common Cause Magazine,* January/February 1990. Available from Common Cause, 2030 M St. NW, Washington, DC 20036.

James A. Dorn and William A. Niskanen — *Dollars, Deficits, and Trade.* Norwell, MA: Kluwen Academic Publishers, 1989.

Jack Egan and Robert F. Black — "The Great Global Buying Binge," *U.S. News & World Report,* July 3, 1989.

Edwin A. Finn Jr. — "World Without Borders," *Forbes,* April 17, 1989.

John Holusha — "Beating Japan at Its Own Game," *The New York Times,* July 16, 1989.

John B. Judis — "The Japanese Megaphone," *The New Republic,* January 22, 1990.

John B. Judis — "U.S. Firms Help 'Dump' Trade Protections," *In These Times,* March 21-27, 1990.

Victor K. Kiam — "Fortress Europe 1992? Don't Hold Your Breath," *The Wall Street Journal,* September 11, 1989.

Robert Kuttner — "A Bouquet, Please, for the European Community," *Business Week,* March 5, 1990.

Thomas G. Labrecque — "Strengthening U.S. Export Performance," *Vital Speeches of the Day,* June 1, 1989.

Brink Lindsey — "Trade Secret," *Policy Review,* Winter 1990.

William J. Madia — "Technology and the European Market of 1992," *Vital Speeches of the Day,* February 1, 1990.

Paul Magnusson and Blanca Reimer — "Carla Hills, Trade Warrior," *Business Week,* January 22, 1990.

Phedon Nicolaides — *Liberalizing Trade in Services: Strategies for Success.* New York: Council on Foreign Relations Press for the Royal Institute of International Affairs, 1989.

William A. Niskanen — "The Bully of World Trade," *Orbis,* Fall 1989.

Robert E. Norton — "The Myths of Foreign Investment," *U.S. News & World Report,* May 29, 1989.

Robert N. Noyce — "A Unique Approach Against Trade Violators," *Vital Speeches of the Day,* August 15, 1989.

John Palmer — "Europe 1992: A Socialist Perspective," *New Politics,* vol. II, no. 4. Available from *New Politics,* PO Box 98, Brooklyn, NY 11231.

Art Pine — "Japanese 'Agents of Influence,'" *Los Angeles Times,* January 30, 1990.

William Pomeroy — "Steps in Trade Cooperation," *People's Daily World,* February 6, 1990. Available from Long-View Publishing, 239 W. 23rd St., New York, NY 10011.

Jim Powell — "Forget the Crowbar," *Reason,* March 1990.

Ernest H. Preeg — *The American Challenge in World Trade: U.S. Interests in the GATT Multilateral Trading System.* Washington, DC: Center for Strategic & International Studies, 1989.

Jane Bryant Quinn — "Europe: It's Already 1992," *Newsweek,* November 20, 1989.

Peter S. Rashish — "High-Tech Alliance with Europe," *Los Angeles Times,* December 17, 1989.

Robert B. Reich — "Who Is Us?" *Harvard Business Review,* January/February 1990.

William F. Ryan — "Europe '92," *Vital Speeches of the Day,* June 1, 1989.

Rich Thomas — "What You Won't Hear in Paris," *Newsweek,* July 17, 1989.

Robert J. Samuelson — "America for Sale?" *The New Republic,* June 12, 1989.

Ryuzo Sato and Julianne Nelson — *Beyond Trade Friction: Japan-U.S. Economic Relations.* New York: Cambridge University Press, 1989.

Philip H. Trezise — "Japan, the Enemy?" *The Brookings Review,* Winter 1989/90.

Ernest Wistrich — *After 1992: The United States of Europe.* London: Routledge & Kegan Paul, 1989.

index